on track ...
Frank Zappa

every album, every song
1966-1979

Eric Benac

on track ...
Frank Zappa

every album, every song
1966-1979

Eric Benac

SONICBOND

sonicbondpublishing.com

Sonicbond Publishing Limited
www.sonicbondpublishing.co.uk
Email: info@sonicbondpublishing.co.uk

First Published in the United Kingdom 2019
First Published in the United States 2019

British Library Cataloguing in Publication Data:
A Catalogue record for this book is available from the British Library

Copyright Eric Benac 2019

ISBN 978-1-78952-033-0

The rights of Eric Benac to be identified as the authors of this work have been asserted by them in accordance with the Copyright, Designs and patents Act 1988.
All rights reserved. No part of this publication may be reproduced, stored in a retrieval system or transmitted in any form or by any means, electronic, mechanical, photocopying, recording or otherwise, without prior permission in writing from Sonicbond Publishing Limited

Typset in ITC Garamond & ITC Avant Garde Gothic
Printed and bound in England

Graphic design and typesetting: Full Moon Media

Acknowledgements

I would like to thank the website *Zappa Analysis* for all of the unique musical insights it offered. Without the skilled breakdown of these concepts, the book would have turned out much differently. Thanks also go out to Kenneth Joseph Benac, Senior and Bonnie Benac, my parents. Both provided support at various times throughout my life and believed in me, unconditionally.

And I would never have even started this book without the encouragement of Daniel Coffey, a fellow music lover, and a great friend. Thank you to young Phillip Santori for reading through each review as I was writing and keeping me focused on finishing this project.

All love and thanks go to Frank Zappa himself, for the over 100 albums and thousands of compositions that have brought me so much joy over the years. And, finally, thanks to the reader for taking the time to purchase or borrow this book and for reading it. Forgive my personal biases throughout: as always, they are just my opinion and are not meant with disrespect to the artist or the fans.

And to Bruce Hamilton, whom always provides such vigorous debate and analysis and support of my writing and music, I extend very warm salutations.

Would you like to write for Sonicbond Publishing?

At Sonicbond Publishing we are always on the look-out for authors, particularly for our two main series:

On Track. Mixing fact with in depth analysis, the On Track series examines the work of a particular musical artist or group. All genres are considered from easy listening and jazz to 60s soul to 90s pop, via rock and metal.

On Screen. This series looks at the world of film and television. Subjects considered include directors, actors and writers, as well as entire television and film series. As with the On Track series, we balance fact with analysis.

While professional writing experience would, of course, be an advantage the most important qualification is to have real enthusiasm and knowledge of your subject. First-time authors are welcomed, but the ability to write well in English is essential.

Sonicbond Publishing has distribution throughout Europe and North America, and all books are also published in E-book form. Authors will be paid a royalty based on sales of their book.

Further details are available from www.sonicbondpublishing.co.uk. To contact us, complete the contact form there or email info@sonicbondpublishing.co.uk

on track ...
Frank Zappa

Contents

Introduction	9
Frank's Formative Years	11
Freak Out!	13
Absolutely Free	19
Lumpy Gravy	25
We're Only In It For The Money	30
Cruising With Ruben and the Jets	36
Uncle Meat	41
Hot Rats	48
Burnt Weeny Sandwich	53
Weasels Ripped My Flesh	58
Chunga's Revenge	63
Fillmore East	67
200 Motels	71
Just Another Band From L.A.	78
Waka / Jawaka	82
The Grand Wazoo	86
Overnite Sensation	91
Apostrophe (')	97
Roxy And Elsewhere	103
One Size Fits All	109
Bongo Fury	114
Zoot Allures	120
Zappa In New York	126
Studio Tan	132
Sleep Dirt	136
Sheik Yerbouti	141
Orchestral Favorites	146
Joe's Garage	150
What Happened After Joe's Garage?	158

Introduction

The word 'genius' is loaded with a lot of expectations and a very heavy load to bear. Ask any artist who was hailed a genius early in their career how it feels to put out work with that kind of burden. For example, all the music Brian Wilson writes will forever be held up against his genius work of the 1960s, particularly *Pet Sounds* and the later finished *Smile* project. The same problem plagues musicians like Paul McCartney and even jazz players like Miles Davis. Once you've been labeled a genius, you have to keep proving you're a genius or fans and critics will start claiming you've lost it or that you were overrated. Few rock musicians likely felt this pressure – and often suffered from it – more than Frank Zappa.

That said, Zappa is arguably the one musician in rock and roll history who could conceivably be labeled a true genius, one who continually produced quality material and who innovated and changed with the times. While fans will continually debate the quality of his '70s and '80s material, there's no denying that even this later work was written with the kind of sophistication and skill that his rock peers mostly lacked. Simply put: Zappa could do anything he wanted to do. If he felt like writing a three-chord punk rock song, he'd find a way to make it interesting and palpable not only for the average audience but for music scholars. And if he wrote classical music, he could trade in various idioms, including romantic, baroque, and even avant-garde styles that put similar efforts by rock musicians to shame. And when he played jazz, he helped to start a new genre – along with many others – called fusion, though obviously Miles Davis did it sooner.

Beyond his composing skills – which also stretched to folk, country, funk, disco, and much more – Zappa was a talented arranger – one of only a handful of his generation who wrote all of his parts down on paper – and producer who pushed the boundaries of what rock and roll could accomplish. While many of his fast edits and noise styles of the '60s were explored by classical musicians before him, Zappa pushed these sounds into the rock realm and put them on albums that often sold hundreds of thousands of copies. In a sense, he did more to popularize these sounds than their originators.

Zappa was also a consummate guitar player who didn't simply play extended solos to take up space. Though not every solo was made equal, his sense of spontaneous composition at his peak made him one of the most thrilling guitarists of his generation. He mostly avoided the type of indulgent histrionics of other players and invented a new style that others tried to emulate in the future.

Beyond his musical abilities, Zappa was also an often insightful social critic who constantly satirized all that he saw. Though his efforts are occasionally off the mark – or sabotaged by obvious 'doo-doo' jokes designed to get the rubes in the audience to chuckle and buy his albums – his early work is particularly penetrating and meaningful. And while his sexual lyrics of the '70s may be somewhat crude compared to his work in the '60s, he was purposefully pushing the boundaries of acceptance in the form. And although not every song or album was a zinger, Zappa's overall thematic and musical consistency up to and including *Joe's Garage* (and even beyond) is hard to ignore. After this album, he had a strange period in the 1980s when he recorded rock albums with less purpose, difficult classical music, meandering theatrical pieces, and computer music based on the Synclavier. Ever restless until the day he died, Zappa left behind a huge archive from which a wealth of intriguing material is still being drawn.

In this book, we're going to take a look at the musical and lyrical content of each of his albums from 1966 to 1979. Each song will get a brief write up discussing the musical element and – if there is room – the lyrics as well. Not every song's lyrics will be quoted directly, but the basic point behind each will be examined briefly. And in each review, the historical context behind the album will be examined, including what critics and fans thought of the album upon its release.

I'd like to thank Globalia and Zappa Music Analysis for their assistance with this book. The in-depth lyrics and performer credits of Globalia helped immensely while the intimidatingly-rich musical study at Zappa Music Analysis helped me keep track of the more technical elements of the songs. Scattered throughout are a few personal ruminations and historical notes that provide the reader with a more engaging atmosphere. And, when possible, recommendations for later work – many of which are posthumous – are included to give you a better understanding of this period of Zappa's work.

So let's not delay any more – let's jump into the weird and often wonderful world of Frank Zappa. Hopefully, you'll learn something you didn't know from this tome. Don't hesitate to share this information with friends or family members who may be interested.

Frank's Formative Years

Like all great musicians, Zappa did not step into the recording studio to craft a debut without any musical experience. In fact, Frank's musical career started very early and included not just the typical R&B and rock and roll music played by his contemporaries but an immersion in modern classical music from a very young age.

Long before the wild days of the Mothers, Frank Zappa was a drummer in Mission Bay High School listening to R&B, blues, doo-wop, and classical music, particularly Varese and Stravinsky. His discovery of modern classical music began when he tracked down a copy of *The Complete Works of Edgard Varese* and started listening to it alongside his parents' extensive collection of Italian operas (Puccini being a big favorite).

> *Since I didn't have any kind of formal training, it didn't make any difference to me if I was listening to Lightnin' Slim, or a vocal group called the Jewels ..., or Webern, or Varèse, or Stravinsky. To me, it was all good music.*

Varese, in particular, remained critical to Zappa's youthful musical development. At the age of 15, his mother let him call Varese, long-distance, on his birthday. While Varese was not at home at the time, he did later answer a letter written to him by Zappa. This friendly letter – in which Varese invited Zappa to visit him in New York City – was framed and proudly displayed throughout Zappa's life. Frank's musical teacher, William Ballard, noticed the young composer's nascent talent and gave him the chance to arrange and compose two pieces of music with the school's orchestra. These were two pieces that would later show up in more rock-based formats: 'A Pound for a Brown (On the Bus)' and 'Sleeping in a Jar.'

After graduation in 1958, Zappa attended Antelope Valley College and continued his musical experiments. While here, Frank composed one of his few 12-tone pieces of music, 'Waltz for Guitar.' Frank's first decent-paying gig was one of two movie scores. The first of these scores was for a strange movie, *Run Home Slow*, written by his English teacher Don Cerveris. The movie itself didn't get released until 1965, but Zappa recorded it in 1963. Though the film is now mostly remembered for Zappa's music, the gig paid well enough to give him the chance to not only buy an electric guitar but to purchase Pal Recording Studio in Cucamonga and re-name it Studio Z.

After purchasing and opening Studio Z, Zappa married longtime girlfriend Kay Sherman and started a flurry of intense musical operation. He played lead guitar in an R&B cover band, The Boogie Men, and Joe Perrino & the Mellotones while he continued his education at Chaffey Junior College. It was here where Zappa studied harmony and pulled together a big band – eight rock musicians and 20 chamber musicians, and the 55-member Pomona Valley Orchestra – to record *The World's Greatest Sinner* soundtrack. While at Studio

Z with Paul Buff at Studio Z, Zappa – still very much a suit-and-tie kind of guy – recorded various singles. These tunes were lighter bits of surf rock, R&B, and novelty music that didn't make much of an impact. Some are available on the *Cucamonga* collection, released by Rhino Records in 2004. None are essential but do show Frank's increasingly sophisticated melodic and harmonic sense.

It was during the early Studio Z days that Zappa met guys like Don Preston, Bunk Gardner, Buzz Gardner, and Ray Collins, all of whom would play in the Mothers. The peak of this early period was reached in 1963, when Zappa not only wrote songs, like 'Any Way the Wind Blows' but also appeared on *The Steve Allen Show*. Zappa's infamous 'bicycle as an instrument' segment was made up on the spot by Frank in a desperate attempt to catch Allen's attention. It was also during 1963 that Zappa's – to that point – biggest success in orchestral music occurred at Mount St. Mary's College. Zappa spent $300 – a significant sum for the struggling musician – and hired a college orchestra to play his music. The performance was broadcast by a local radio station. Zappa played the zither during this performance, a rarity.

In spite of these formal successes, 1963 also saw his marriage was breaking up, which inspired Zappa to start working 12 or more hours every day on his music. It was in this year that the clueless vice squad group in the area took a newspaper article – in which he was dubbed 'the Movie King of Cucamonga' – as proof that he was making porn. An undercover officer contacted Zappa about making a stag tape for a party. Zappa – who was offered nearly $800 in today's money – quickly threw together the tape with a female friend. The two made exaggerated sexual noises, jumped on a bed, and had a hard time not laughing at the whole thing. Unfortunately, the vice squad arrested Zappa. The trial – during which the attending judge laughed out loud at the tape – resulted in Zappa getting six months in jail but serving only 10 days. In the resulting raid on Studio Z, he lost 50 of an estimated 80 hours of tapes. Eviction from the studio followed before it was torn down in 1966. The moment was a critical one for the young man and fueled the lifelong distrust of authority that inspired his long and intense career.

Freak Out! (1966)
Personnel:
Frank Zappa: composer, guitar, conductor, vocals
Jimmy Carl Black: percussion, drums, vocals
Ray Collins: vocals, harmonica, cymbals, sound effects, tambourine, finger cymbals, bobby pin & tweezers
Roy Estrada: bass, guitarrón, boy soprano
Elliot Ingber: alternate lead & rhythm guitar with clear white light
Recorded between March 9 and March 12, 1966
Released on June 27, 1966
Producer: Tom Wilson with arrangements by Frank Zappa
Engineer: Ami, Tom, and Val Valentin
Peak Position: US Billboard Chart: 130

In many ways, *Freak Out!* is the definitive Zappa album. Though mostly critically lambasted upon its release, it was an underground cult smash and has become regarded as one of the best albums of all time. For example, 2003 placed it on their '500 Greatest Albums of All Time' list at 243, a spot in the 2006 book *1001 Albums You Must Hear Before You Die*, and a place in Classic Rock magazine's '50 Albums That Built Prog Rock.' And in 1999, it received a Grammy.

These accolades are more than deserved. Though it lacks some of Zappa's later composition and arrangement intricacy, it successfully synthesizes every element of his music. There are rock songs with doo-wop vocals, talking blues songs with satirical lyrics, difficult avant pieces based on percussion sounds, brief glimpses of scatological humor, and experiments in sound that still resonate over 50 years later. The amazing thing about this album is that it comes from the hands of such inauspicious players. The early Mothers of Invention originated as a cover group, The Soul Giants, that Zappa joined as a guitar player through the friendship of singer Ray Collins. Zappa tried to get the R&B-oriented band to perform his originals, claiming that they would make the group famous. Original leader and saxophone player Davy Coronado did not agree and left under pressure from the rest of the band.

The Soul Giants were unique because of their multi-racial lineup, as Jimmy Carl Black was a Native American and Roy Estrada was a Mexican American. Later on, in the band's career, Estrada would lament this fact because he believed that the band lost gigs due to his racial background, a fear later parodied on the live album *Ahead of Their Time*, a 1968 show released in 1993. Zappa convinced the band to move to Los Angeles in early 1965 and found them a contract with Herb Cohen, who found them consistent club work. During this period, Zappa worked to transform the primitive playing of his band. As the band's reputation grew, their behavior became more outrageous. For example, the term The Mothers is a shortened version of 'motherfuckers,' a compliment given to great bands. Zappa later had this to say about the band name:

> *...it was kind of presumptuous to name the band that, because we weren't that good musicians...by bar-band standards in the area, we were light-years ahead of our competition, but in terms of real musicianship, I just suppose we were right down there in the swamp*

Regardless, the band's unique improvisational chemistry mixed with Zappa's originals to create an increasingly popular live experience. Their reputation caused Tom Wilson of MGM to check out a gig. He had the chance to hear 'Trouble Every Day' and was suitably impressed to offer them a record deal with Verve Records in 1966. Once the band started recording, Wilson quickly realized that he had signed something much different than a blues band. The band recorded the upbeat ballad 'Any Way the Wind Blows' and followed it up with the heavy and bizarre 'Who Are the Brain Police?' which was years ahead of its time. Zappa later joked that he saw Wilson '...scrambling toward the phone to call his boss – probably saying: "Well, uh, not exactly a 'white blues band', but ... sort of."'

Wilson said: 'Zappa, without exception, is the biggest talent I have ever come across...' and when asked if the band were a 'joke' stated that 'They are a joke to this extent in that they – and Frank in particular – regard the pop music of the '50s on which the current Anglo-American pop scene is largely based, as a joke.' His statement is spot on, as a large portion of the songs recorded for the album were satirical parodies. However, this is no Weird Al album (as much as I love Mr. Yankovich). Each song is written flawlessly, with gorgeous melodies and strong lyrics. And though there is a strong streak of parody and satire on the album, songs like 'Anyway the Wind Blows' are based on real-life experiences, as Zappa wrote that song to ease his pain during his divorce. And while the Mothers of Invention played the backing tracks with skill and aplomb, a large number of guest musicians were brought in to expand the sound. Many members of the skilled Wrecking Crew, such as Carole Kaye and Mac Rebennack (Dr. John) contributed.

Sometime later, Kaye would claim that only 'the drummer and bass player,' i.e., Estrada and Black, played on the album while the guitar work was handled by the Wrecking Crew. It seems unlikely that Zappa and Ingber didn't play at all, though clearly much 12-string guitar was added by Kaye and other musicians. Kaye, however, did praise Zappa and claimed that, of all the rock musicians in Los Angeles, only he and Brian Wilson wrote their own arrangements. Orchestral embellishments were added to several songs, all playing with Zappa arrangements and under his supervision. This freedom provided Zappa with the chance to express himself on just about every song. This type of goodwill did not extend to future albums, however, and even ended on this album as the band was denied more studio time to finish 'The Return of the Son of Monster Magnet.'

A huge promotional push by the label resulted in sales disappointment (a mere 130 spot on the Billboard Chart), critical aggression, and listener indifference. However, other musicians were listening. For example, Paul McCartney later stated that *Sgt. Peppers* was The Beatles' version of *Freak Out!* And at 60 minutes, it was one of the first double albums and the very first double-album debut by a rock band. The record's influence would seep into the burgeoning hippie culture and gave Zappa the impetus he needed to expand his sound even further.

'Hungry Freaks Daddy' (Frank Zappa)
This sharp opening track reveals the depth of Zappa's writing and arranging skills. The layered opening guitar parts are not only memorable but playing harmonic, rather than unison, lines. The verses feature Zappa singing mournful lyrics regarding the indifference of older generations. Though mostly based on guitar, touches of vibraphone pop up. The structure of this song is not verse-chorus-verse but features a refrain at the end of each verse. Each verse is taken in a different key to give the song more musical variation. And the presence of kazoos during the refrain adds an unpredictable, surreal, and silly touch.

'I Ain't Got No Heart' (Frank Zappa)
The sharp-tongued parodies begin with this track, which features an amazing first verse:

I sit and laugh at fools in love
There ain't no such thing as love
No angels singing up above today

In a time when a majority of pop and rock music focused heavily on love thematic themes, this direct attack still resounds. The excellent opening riff replays and shifts through a few keys. The bridge features a touch of psychedelic-like screams and droning vocals over heavy acid guitar. And when the orchestra pops up to embellish the ending melodic themes, it's not hard to feel like you've been on a prog-like journey in a mere 2:34!

'Who are the Brain Police' (Frank Zappa)
This song is a sharp departure from previous songs, one that Zappa claimed came to him in a dream. It features lyrics such as 'What will you do if we let you go home and the plastic's all melted and so is the chrome? Who are the brain police?' This type of paranoia was brewing across the '60s rock scene but came to an early peak here.

The music mostly consists of drones and dirges that became popular with later musicians, but while these psychedelic wanderers claimed influence from Indian and Middle Eastern music, Zappa's seem rooted in more traditional Western theory. The song takes a drastic turn with a 'pounding and screaming' bridge similar to 'I Ain't Got No Heart.'

'Go Cry on Somebody Else's Shoulder' (Frank Zappa and Ray Collins)
Zappa's love of doo-wop balladry comes to the fore. Though the lyrics retain a satirical edge, the melody is intricate and catchy enough to be a standard and features the same type of varied writing and arrangement that is typical of Zappa. For example, there are more instruments on this song than you would find in a typical doo-wop standard. There are some guitar countermelodies and piano parts but, in spite of these embellishments, this is one of the more straightforward songs here.

'Motherly Love' (Frank Zappa)
'Motherly Love' was the fourth single released from *Freak Out!* and is one of a handful originally recorded in 1965 for a demo. Other songs on this demo – released in 2004 on the *Joe's Corsage* album – include 'I Ain't Got No Heart.' This version of 'Motherly Love' is more elaborate with kazoos, differing melodies, and a harder guitar tone than earlier versions. The lyrics are disguised '60s smut – groupies, come and bask in the raw sexual power of Frank's band of merry misfits!

'How Could I Be Such a Fool?' (Frank Zappa)
Side one ends with one of Frank's most intricate ballads. The verses continually build, including gorgeous arpeggios, before coming to a halt on the chorus with sustained vibes and a sense of space unique for Zappa. Horn countermelodies and layered 12-string guitars on the post-chorus thicken the sound considerably. And the ending horn flourish brings in a light touch of jazz. The attention to arrangement details and the sense of songwriting skill displayed here put Zappa ahead of most of his peers.

'Wowie Zowie' (Frank Zappa)
Side two of *Freak Out!* features some of the more 'commercial' sounds on the album. For example, 'Wowie Zowie' features dancing vibes, wide-eyed musical innocence, and a bubble gum pop atmosphere thrown off guard by lyrics like 'I don't even care if your dad's the heat.' I can imagine sipping a root beer float at the local sock hop while this tune plays.

'You Didn't Try to Call Me' (Frank Zappa)
Another excellent, concise, and artfully-written and arranged pop song that integrates various melodies, instrumental parts, and keys into a hard-hitting whole. Listening to these short, constantly evolving – but never busy – songs really highlights how much influence Zappa had on the art-rock of the time, particularly in the way he so skillfully shifts keys, tempo, and time signatures.

'Any Way the Wind Blows' (Frank Zappa)
Another excellent doo-wop-inspired rock song with personal lyrics expressing Zappa's emotional confusion at the end of his first marriage. Many of the same arrangement and compositional tricks utilized throughout the album are also implemented here. Not a lot to say except that it's another example of Zappa's pop songwriting skill.

'I'm Not Satisfied' (Frank Zappa)
Deep doo-wop vocals, intricate vocal melodies, and surprisingly angst-filled lyrics highlight one of Frank's more personal songs:

> *Got no place to go*
> *I'm tired of walking up and down the street all by myself*
> *No love left for me to give*
> *I try and try but no-one wants me the way I am*

The horn embellishments are particularly skilled in a beautiful piece of suicide-pop years ahead of its time in its surprisingly sensitive subject matter.

'You're Probably Wondering Why I'm Here' (Frank Zappa)
The interesting stop-start structure of the verses contrasts with more driving sections that serve as a musical chorus hook. The kazoos come back in full force here, and those lyrics? Classic!

> *You rise each day the same old way*
> *And join your friends out on the street*
> *Spray your hair*
> *And think you're neat*
> *I think your life is incomplete*
> *But maybe that's not for me to say*
> *They only pay me here to play*

'Trouble Every Day' (Frank Zappa)
Side three is where things start getting very strange. Interestingly, the first song lineup for the album started with 'Trouble Every Day' rather than consigning it late on the album. Zappa and Wilson clearly thought a lot of the song and its electric talking blues. The lyrics are among Zappa's sharpest written and remain relevant. It's one of the few songs he performed to the very end of his career. A typical example of its insights include:

> *Wednesday I watched the riot*
> *I seen the cops out on the street*
> *I watched 'em throwin' rocks & stuff & chokin'*

> *In the heat*
> *I listen to reports*
> *'Bout the whisky passin' around*
> *I seen the smoke & fire*
> *And the market burnin' down*
> *I watched while everybody*
> *On his street would take a turn*
> *To stomp & smash & bash & crash & slash & bust & burn*

The music features a few classic Zappa touches, including the upbeat chorus section and the mournful, and echoing guitar. The textures and lyrics are a poignant reminder that Zappa was not a gimmick and that he could write emotional music.

'Help, I'm a Rock' (Frank Zappa)

Zappa's first extended piece remains one of his strangest. Technically, it is a 'suite in three movements,' but the music mostly maintains a similar tone. The tune starts out with a simple, but unnerving, hammered-on guitar riff echoed on multiple instruments. The lyrics are indescribable: 'You know, maybe I should become a police officer. Help, I'm a cop! Help I'm a cop!' Various strange voices – most by Roy Estrada – float in and out of the mix to create a disturbing atmosphere. No other song on the album is quite as odd or off-putting as this incredible tune.

'The Return of the Son of Monster Magnet (Unfinished Ballet in Two Tableaux)' (Frank Zappa)

With the now-infamous opening dialogue between Zappa and Susie Creamcheese, this composition takes up nearly one-fifth of the whole album. The pounding drums and odd synthesizer noises bring Zappa's Varese fixation into clearer focus. The lyrics, what few are here, are very satirical. 'America is wonderful! Wonderful! Wonderful! Wonderful!'

Unfortunately, the track was designed to be more intricate and detailed, including layers of instruments and was to be the 'pull-out-all-the-stops' ending to the album. However, MGM – who had already put an astonishing $25,000-30,000 into the album – refused additional studio time or funding, leaving the song in a barebone state. While it remains intriguing, the full potential of the song is fascinating to consider.

Absolutely Free (1967)

Personnel:
Frank Zappa: guitar, conductor, and vocals
Jimmy Carl Black: drums, and vocals
Ray Collins: vocals, tambourine, harmonica, and prune (?)
Roy Estrada: bass and vocals
Billy Mundi: drums and percussion
Don Preston: keyboards
Jim Fielder: guitar, piano
Bunk Gardner: woodwinds
Recorded between November 15-18, 1966
Released on May 26, 1967
Produced by: Tom Wilson.
Engineered by: Ami Hadani
Peak Chart Position: Number 41 on the US Billboard 200

The lack of huge commercial success for *Freak Out!* triggered a few reactions from the Zappa camp. MGM set a strict budget of $11,000 for *Absolutely Free*, which limited the amount of time the band could spend polishing it up. As a result, there are a few obvious mistakes and flubs, which is understandable, considering the expanded scope and ambition. An increased focus on unpredictable musicianship and classical and jazz-based composition styles were likely influenced by the relative failure of *Freak Out!* Freed from what Zappa no doubt considered the shackles of writing hit pop songs, he could pursue his own vision.

The concept for the album was to create two suites of music that each covered one side of a record (each labeled a 'Series of Underground Oratorios'). Groundbreaking at the time, this style would influence future bands making sweeping statements. And while the attempt is relatively crude in execution, the quality of the music remains high.

The first side of the album is an absurdist exploration of vegetables (among other things) while the second is a scathing look at the absurdity of modern American life. The addition of keyboardist Don Preston, woodwinds player Buck Gardner, guitarist Jim Fielder, and drummer Billy Mundi expanded the Mothers' range, though the Wrecking Crew appears on a limited basis. Fielder was in the band so briefly that his name was removed from the credits. He later went on to play in Blood, Sweat, and Tears, Buffalo Springfield, and with Neil Sedaka. The relative lack of guitar here – most intricate instrumental sections are played either by Gardner or Preston – may explain why Fielder was such a short-term member of the band.

If Fielder was put off by the lack of guitar on the songs, imagine how much of Zappa's audience reacted. Gone were the rich and colorful pop songs of *Freak Out!* and, in their place, were songs with rapidly-changing structures, intricate ensemble playing, and constantly changing keys and time signatures. As a result, *Absolutely Free* has the feel of psychedelic music but with musicianship that far surpasses the sometimes (pleasantly) crude playing of other groups. The overall feel is a bit like the collage-style of *Abbey Road* but with more detailed playing, faster-changing parts, and a lot more people screaming about prunes at the top of their lungs. Not to say it's better than the Beatles' late-period masterpiece: just similar in approach.

The complete change of tone and approach were a big hit with the underground audience, as *Absolutely Free* rose as high as 41 on the Billboard Pop Charts. This surprising level of success emboldened Frank to continue following his own muse, no matter how much record companies balked.

'Plastic People' (Frank Zappa)
The band originally played this song live by hammering on that three-chord 'Louie, Louie' riff for all it was worth. In this expanded version, Gardner and Preston give the Mothers the ability to play with time signatures, stops-and-starts, and experimental chords. The lyrics are typical Zappa satire:

> *She's as plastic*
> *As she can be*
> *She paints her face*
> *With plastic goo*
> *And wrecks her hair*
> *With some shampoo*

The pop of *Freak Out!* is dropped as the band focuses on the improvisational textures they would sketch out over the next few years. The song abruptly segues to the next track to begin the collage-like feel used on both sides of the album.

'The Duke of Prunes' (Frank Zappa)
Frank's past catches up with him here: by taking the gorgeous love theme from *Run Home Slow* and pairing it with absurdist lyrics ('I see your lovely beans, and in your magic go-kart, I bite your neck'), he crafts a wonderful song. Gardner is particularly critical to the beginning, as his woodwinds generate a late-night atmosphere. During the second section, the melody is played with a rock-oriented feel, with the dual drumming of Black and Mundi creating a percussive drive. Zappa's guitar work is restrained with a handful of tight bluesy guitar breaks. Ultimately, the track resolves and transitions to the next.

'Amnesia Vivace' (Frank Zappa, Igor Stravinsky)
This one-minute instrumental is the first showcase of Zappa's Stravinsky fixation. The segment 'Ritual Action of the Ancestors' from The Rite of Spring, Part II is played before Preston plays 'Dance of the Adolescents' in Part I, before

transitioning to Berceuse. Vocals are mostly limited to Frank chanting 'Duke, Duke, Duke, Duke of Prunes' to the melody of 'Duke of Earl.'

'The Duke Regains His Chops' (Frank Zappa)
A variation of the rock section of 'The Duke of Prunes' with more pronounced bass and guitar. Somebody shouts 'New Cheese!' as the band chants 'chaka, chaka, chaka, chaka,' and 'the love I have for you will never end...well maybe!' on top of tight rock and roll guitar lines. Frank jokes 'This is the exciting part. This is like the Supremes, see the way it builds up?' as the chords rise higher and higher and Estrada howls in the background like a maniac. Psychedelic music made by a man who hated psychedelic music. As cool as it gets.

'Call Any Vegetable' (Frank Zappa)
Another absurdist ode to our plant friends, 'Call Any Vegetable' features one of my favorite Zappa asides: 'Some people don't go for prunes, I don't know, I've always found that if they...' The arrangement is based on pounding drums and bass with a clarinet for the main melody. The guitar is used strictly for rhythm. 'Rutabaga, rutabaga, rutabaga, rutabaga' before jumping into a rather intricate countermelody section with harpsichord and woodwind dancing and harmonizing. It all builds up to a climax before abruptly switching to the next track. Later versions slowed the track down and focused more on guitar. Some prefer that version: I do not.

'Invocation and Ritual Dance of the Young Pumpkin' (Frank Zappa, Gustav Holst)
The first extended Mothers jam on record might not be their best but has a lot going on. Zappa's growing skill on the guitar is showcased with some sharp, concise, and biting solos that play off Gardner's saxophone very well. Plenty of difficult unison playing, tempo increases, cadences, and much more highlight a track that gives listeners an insight into what to expect at the typical Mothers' show. More classical music abounds, as Holst's 'Jupiter, the Bringer of Jollity' is referenced in Gardner's sax solo.

'Soft-Sell Conclusion' (Frank Zappa, Stravinsky)
This track serves as a soft landing pad for the end of side one. 'A lot of people don't bother with their friends in the vegetable kingdom...' Another Stravinsky quote: the ending theme is the opening melody of 'Marche Royale.' More stop-and-start tightness with Gardner and Preston coloring the music with finesse and skill. A harmonica pops up for a few bars. The collage-style approach remains strong in this song's sub-two-minute length.

'America Drink' (Frank Zappa)
Silly acapella nonsense starts before a clarinet, bass, and vocals intone a strange

melody. A few flubs are present here, in a charming way. At 1:20, the tone changes as the drums enter and Preston kicks in with some harpsichord stabs. More clarinet and booming noises before the next track begins.

'Status Back Baby' (Frank Zappa)

This track is a slice-of-life look at the average high school teenager. The rhythm guitar, drums, and bass keep things punchy while Collins describes the protagonist's inability to stay cool at school. You get heroic guitar sounds, whistles, and clarinets playing scale-based arpeggios. There is also some more twisted chording on the guitar that follows the strange noise bridge – a favorite trick of Zappa's at the time – before the last verse kicks into a slightly higher key. With a bit more polish and straighter lyrics, it could have been a hit.

'Uncle Bernie's Farm' (Frank Zappa)

A slightly groove-based tune that features plenty of acid-like guitar mixed with high-pitched keyboard sounds. The concept of plasticity comes back into play as Zappa writes some of the harshest and hard-hitting lyrics on the album:

> *There's a little plastic congress*
> *There's a nation you can buy, I'll take two*
> *There's a doll that looks like mommy*
> *She'll do anything but cry*
> *There's a doll that looks like daddy*
> *He's a funny little man*
> *Push a button & ask for money*
> *There's a dollar in his hand, check his wallet*

The transition to the 'we gotta send Santa Claus back to the rescue mission' segment is a bit awkward, but the move back to the main melodic section works just fine, as Zappa digs even deeper:

> *There's a man who runs the country*
> *There's a man who tried to think*
> *And they're all made out of plastic*
> *When they melt they start to stink*
> *There's a book with smiling children*
> *Nearly dead with Christmas joys!*
> *And smiling in his office*
> *Is the creep who makes the toys*

'Son of Suzy Creamcheese' (Frank Zappa)

A fine guitar-based rocker that brings back Suzy from the last album. After the hard-hitting 'Uncle Bernie's Farm,' the silliness here is a relief. The somewhat straighter style also sets the listener up for one of the best tracks Zappa ever wrote.

'Brown Shoes Don't Make It' (Frank Zappa)
Though the rest of the album is a trip, Zappa pulls out all the stops on this track. The title, based on the time Lyndon B. Johnson wore a pair of ugly shoes with a gray suit (don't ask), Frank's condemnation of American society reaches a, sometimes ugly, peak. Sample lyrics include:

> *A world of secret hungers*
> *Perverting the men who make your laws*
> *Every desire is hidden away*
> *In a drawer... in a desk*
> *By a Naugahyde chair*
> *On a rug where they walk and drool*
> *Past the girls in the office*

Composed of no less than eight musical segments, 'Brown Shoes Don't Make It' feels like *Absolutely Free* as a whole crammed into eight minutes. There are rock segments, strange classical pieces, droning psychedelic moods, modern classical tonal poems, strutting R&B, doo-wop, bubblegum singalongs, avant noise, and mad swing.

'Brown Shoes' is fantastic and is among the most complex and unpredictable tracks of the '60s. The band plays each section quite well, with Gardner, Preston, and Estrada sounding particularly nice. Though things don't flow as smoothly as later Zappa epics (you can practically hear the scissors cutting through the tape), 'Brown Shoes' remains a classic.

'America Drinks and Goes Home' (Frank Zappa)
After the sprawl and social critique of the previous track, Zappa and the band play a little lounge music. Ray Collins is particularly fine as a jazz crooner while Preston plays some excellent jazzy runs. Overdubbed audience and cash register noises create a sleazy live feel. Collins then starts addressing the audience directly, talking about dance nights, twist contests, 'giving away peanut butter and jelly bologna sandwiches to all of ya' and playing 'Caravan with a drum sola.' As the song winds to an end, the listener is likely scratching their head in confusion at this deflating turn – not the last that Zappa would utilize.

Bonus Tracks
'Big Leg Emma' and 'Why Don'tcha Do Me Right?' (Frank Zappa)
'Big Leg Emma' and 'Why Don'tcha Do Me Right?' are rather awkwardly shoved between the first and second sides of the album on the official Barking Pumpkin CD re-release. The former is a well-composed, if slightly misogynist,

ode to a beautiful girl who lost her looks. The second is a droning guitar rocker that feels unique in Zappa's discography at the time. Both were singles released around the same time as the album that bombed. Wisely, the 2017 vinyl reissue places these tracks on the bonus LP to restore the album's original flow.

Lumpy Gravy (1967/68)
Personnel:
Abnuceals Emuukha Electric Symphony Orchestra, including:
Jimmy Carl Black: chorus
Louis 'Louie the Turkey' Cuneo: chorus
Roy Estrada – bass and chorus
Larry Fanoga aka Euclid James 'Motorhead' Sherwood: vocals and chorus
Victor Feldman: percussion and drums
Bunk Gardner: woodwinds
Bruce Hampton: chorus
Tommy Tedesco: guitar
Frank Zappa: composer, conductor, arranger
Many more orchestral and chorus members
Initial Orchestral Recordings: February 13 and March 14-16, 1967
Released on August 7, 1967 (orchestra-only version) and May 13, 1968 (full version)
Producer: Frank Zappa
Engineers: Gary Kellgren, Dick Kunc
Editing: Dick Kunc, Frank Zappa
Peak Chart Position: Number 159 on the US Billboard 200

After two rock albums for Verve, Zappa was contacted by Nick Venet of Capitol Records and commissioned to write a suite of orchestral music. Zappa was thrilled – he'd been longing to record some 'serious' music – but ran into a slight problem. Verve had him under contract as a performer, including the Mothers of Invention, so the album could not feature him as a performer.

The solution? The album would be released under his name – Verve did not have a contract for his solo albums – and he wouldn't perform. Instead, Frank would compose and conduct a band featuring multiple studio rock musicians and a large orchestra. Three Mothers played on the album: Buck Gardner, Roy Estrada, and Motorhead. The liners also state that Bruce Hampton – of the Hampton Grease Band – sang in the chorus on the album. As a huge fan of that group, I had never read this interesting fact. Anyone who likes Zappa and Beefheart should check out their classic double album *Music to Eat* for some intricate guitar-based Zappa-style rock and roll.

Anyway, Venet was a true believer and served as a producer alongside Frank while pumping in $40,000 into the project. The piece was composed in 11 days and was conceived of as a Cage-inspired oratorio, and was 22 minutes long. The recording sessions took place over a handful of days and may have gone faster had the musicians known what to expect.

The orchestra did not, initially, take the project seriously. Percussionist Emil Richards was amused that a guitarist in a rock band was trying such a serious project. He anticipated that Zappa would be completely lost or would rely on outside arrangers. However, Frank handed him lengthy sheet notes with dense and complex music filled with difficult melodies and multiple time signatures. Richards' friend, guitarist Tommy Tedesco, also believed that Zappa was clueless and was only convinced that he was the real deal when the project was finished. Part of this newfound belief was influenced by a playing conflict. The bassoonist and bass clarinetist took one look at Frank's score and – under the impression that he was a buffoon – declared their parts unplayable. Zappa calmly stated: 'If I play your part, will you at least try it?' After he nailed the parts on the guitar, they admitted defeat.

This original version was released on August 7, 1967, but had to be quickly withdrawn after the expected lawsuit from MGM, the owner of Verve. After the album was withdrawn, Zappa took it into the studio and edited it, adding new elements such as spoken word parts, musique concrete transitions, and even a surf rock song he'd originally recorded in his Studio Z days. The new album was then released on May 13, 1968, to limited commercial success. Reviews either praised Zappa's ambition and execution or lamented that the album wasn't quite what they'd hoped. Jim Miller of Rolling Stone wrote:

> Yet in spite of its varied tricks, **Lumpy Gravy** does not come to life; it is a strangely sterile recording, as though all the studio musicians reading their music could not do what a batch of well-rehearsed Mothers can do...The texture of the music (and the scoring of the instruments, for that matter) is surprisingly conventional and even boring...

In spite of the mixed response, Zappa was very proud and called it one of his favorites. It was recorded simultaneously with *We're Only In It for the Money* and was part of the extended *No Commercial Potential* project which featured those two albums, *Cruising With Ruben and the Jets*, and the *Uncle Meat* movie and soundtrack. The result took Zappa's collage-style approach to a bursting point and showed the world that he could write and arrange real orchestral music. And while Miller's complaints of conventional scoring do hold some weight, the movement and feel of the piece remain original and striking.

Note: Dialogue outtakes were later used in the Synclavier magnum opus, *Civilization Phaze III*. The original orchestra-only version of the album was not heard again in full until the box set, *Lumpy Money*, was released in 2009 alongside the full 1985 edit featuring newly-composed vocal parts. Note that the tracks listed below are not indexed on most CD recordings but used as general indicators of the various segments of sides one and two of the 1968 *Lumpy Gravy*.

'The Way I See It, Barry' (Frank Zappa)
Very brief vocal introduction in which someone (Zappa?) says 'the way I see it, Barry, tonight should be a very dynamite show.'

'Duodenum' (Frank Zappa)
The first extended melodic movement on the album was often referred to as the 'Lumpy Gravy Theme' when played live. It includes members of both the rock and orchestral group and has a surf-rock feel mixed with horns and strings The 1985 version featured Ike Willis singing 'duodenum' to little effect.

'Oh No' (Frank Zappa)
One of Frank's most beloved melodies. Stated mostly on vibes and guitar, it alternates 4/4 and 3/4 sections quite smoothly. The overall feel has a chamber-like texture that is pleasing and a nice setup for the abrasive nature of future sections.

'Bit of Nostalgia' (Frank Zappa)
This segment begins with a few seconds of surf rock (to serve as the 'bit of nostalgia for the old folks') before a pretty dense sound collage.

'It's From Kansas' (Frank Zappa)
One of the wilder bits of music from the first side, 'It's From Kansas' is a piece of sped-up music that constantly changes scales while holding a standard beat. The music is, in essence, a fairly traditional rendering of pre-war jazz executed in a frantic way.

'Bored Out 90 Over' (Frank Zappa)
A dialogue section that features brief bits of music. The standout part is the 'Louie, Louie' interjection that makes this writer laugh out loud. The rambling and nonsensical discussions of life in California and the search for the 'Big Note' are either entertaining or exasperating, depending on the listener.

'Almost Chinese' (Frank Zappa)
This brief melody emulates Eastern musical styles by playing a simple chord progression that drops the third of every chord to play in parallel fourths. This achieves a pseudo-'Chinese' sound, hence the title.

'Switching Girls' (Frank Zappa)
More dialogue, this time about changing girlfriends.

'Oh No Again' (Frank Zappa)
The reprise of 'Oh No' features a slightly different arrangement and tempo for a sense of conceptual continuity. After two more lengthy dialogue pieces ('At the Gas Station' and 'Another Pickup') the last segment of side one begins.

'I Don't Know If I Can Go Through This Again' (Frank Zappa)
Frank's Varese and Stravinsky influences pop up over this four-minute track. Atonal bits of flute and orchestral meanderings create a surprisingly strong

effect that is one of the best moments on the album. The side then ends with a lovely orchestrated piece to minimize psychological damage.

'Very Distraughtening' (Frank Zappa)
More piano-people dialogue focused on pigs and ponies and the 'Big Note' theory. Brief snatches of electronic music appear throughout to upset listener expectations. Bits of distorted and sped-up rock tunes play very quietly to end the track. References to Larry 'Wildman' Fischer appear here ('Merry Go Round').

'White Ugliness' (Frank Zappa)
More dialogue nonsense starring Louis 'Louie the Turkey' Cuneo describing two 'boogeymen' fighting him. The 'pickup sticks' segment is funny enough, but Louis' indescribable laugh might be the defining element of the whole album.

'Amen' (Frank Zappa)
A prayer to Motorhead heralds this avant piece. Consisting of tumbling percussion, plunking pianos, and sudden swells in sound, 'Amen' feels like the music Zappa would be writing and conducting for *200 Motels*. There is a lot of dense, atonal, and dissonant string writing here.

'Just One More Time' (Frank Zappa)
This segment begins with a very Beefheart-sounding singer intoning the title over circus-style organ music. It then falls into more dialogue, including a rambling discourse on 'saluting the smoke' as a basis of nationalism that still feels accurate today.

'A Vicious Cycle' (Frank Zappa)
More sped-up tape madness featuring composed bits and dense improvisation. The increased tempo makes things feel wilder. After somebody blandly states 'pony,' the music falls into string-based plucking with no tonal center. More dissonant orchestral segments appear throughout, utilizing strict parallel thirds.

'King Kong' (Frank Zappa)
The first recorded version of this classic is taken at a slower tempo than the *Uncle Meat* take. By liberally mixing rock and classical instruments, Zappa continues to surprise. The overall feel here is lackadaisical, and there may be mistakes due to the time crunch. That said, you get some of Frank's best counterpoint composition here, including a surprising break into 4/4 time.

'Drums are Too Noisy' (Frank Zappa)
A brief segment of mostly percussive noises. Multiple drum parts play at the same time while the piano, vibraphone, and bass are used as percussion, not melodic, instruments. This creates a free jazz feel that transitions to dialogue.

'Kangaroos' (Frank Zappa)
This short piece is surprisingly complex. There are six variations of a theme stated and expanded upon over two 5/4 bars. There is no centering tone, and the music increases in volume and intensity over each variation. It combines to create one of the most successful pieces of modern music on the album.

'It Envelops the Bathtub' (Frank Zappa)
More modern classical with a strong sense of space, this track progresses from woodwind melodies to a drum-based segment that feels free. Movement is implied, rather than stated, through vibraphone and woodwind melodies. As one of the longest intact segments from the first edition of *Lumpy Gravy*, this track features some of its most complex and detailed writing. The counterpoint and harmonies are dense while the instrumentation and arrangements continually shift.

'Take Your Clothes Off' (Frank Zappa)
On the soon to be released *We're Only In It for the Money*, 'Take Your Clothes Off When You Dance' would be a wonderful melodic highlight. The lyrics would feature a semi-mocking declaration of the power of freedom and love. This very Dick Hyman-like instrumental arrangement includes guitar, organ, intentionally cheesy 'la la la' vocals, and surf-style drumming. It is a fun and unpredictable way to end the album.

We're Only In It for the Money (1968)
Personnel:
Frank Zappa: guitar, piano, lead vocals, and 'weirdness & editing'
Dick Barber: ('snorks')
Jimmy Carl Black: 'Indian of the group', drums, trumpet, and vocals
Roy Estrada: electric bass, vocals, and 'asthma'
Bunk Gardner: all woodwinds, and 'mumbled weirdness'
Billy Mundi: drums, vocal, and 'yak & black lace underwear'
Don Preston: keyboards
Euclid James Motorhead Sherwood: soprano saxophones, baritone saxophones, and 'all-purpose weirdness'
Ian Underwood: piano, woodwinds, and 'wholesome'
Pamela Zarubica: Suzy Creamcheese on the 'telephone'
Producer: Frank Zappa
Executive Producer: Tom Wilson
Engineers: Gary Kellgren, Dick Kunc
Recorded: March 14–16, August 2–9, and October 1967
Released on March 4, 1968
Peak Chart Position: Number 30 on the US Billboard 200

We're Only In It for the Money remains a remarkable and unforgettable listen 50 years after its release. The album is not just a satire of the burgeoning hippie movement but a condemnation of the society that triggered its rise. Zappa's lyrical and satirical wit reach heights he rarely topped again: give him something to rave against, and Frank could be the most intelligent social observer in rock.

The bitterness and angst directed at hippies here are somewhat personal. Frank viewed himself as something of a leader of the 'freaks,' a group of outcasts and underground individuals who later tumbled over into the hippie scene. His view of bands jumping on the bandwagon of psychedelic or 'art' music (particularly the Beatles) was that they were 'only in it for the money'. Beyond that, he wanted to position himself as the real leader of the youth movement, which he felt was being exploited and commercialized. Of his band, Zappa put it bluntly in the title of his work during this period, which fell under the collective heading of *No Commercial Potential*. He said:

> *It's all one album. All the material in the albums is organically related and if I had all the master tapes and I could take a razor blade and cut them apart and put it together again in a different order it still would make one piece of music you can listen to. Then I could take that razor blade and cut it apart and reassemble it a different way, and it still would make sense.*

Though the music here is among Frank's most melodic – including moments of touching beauty – there were demands for censorship. For example, Verve asked that Zappa remove the final verse from 'Mother People,' which he reversed and added to 'Hot Poop.' He was also forced to remove a segment in 'Concentration Moon' in which engineer Gary Kellgren – who does the whispered vocal parts throughout the album – calls The Velvet Underground a 'shitty' band. Thankfully, Zappa's continuing fascination with the studio as an instrument continued. Tracks abruptly cut off to play random gibberish. Layered orchestral music from *Lumpy Gravy* occur throughout, and the segue style of *Absolutely Free* was fine-tuned. And Frank's dedication to doing his own thing was rewarded with a top Billboard placing of 30.

Note: In 1984, Zappa edited this album, *Cruising With Ruben and the Jets*, and *Lumpy Gravy,* adding new bass guitar (Arthur Barrow) and drum (Chad Wackerman) parts and new vocal parts added by Ike Willis on *Lumpy Gravy*. Though the playing and singing was well done, both stand out like sore thumbs on the mix. Later CD releases restored the original instrumentation, though the original *Ruben* mix was thought lost and not restored until the *Greasy Love Songs* set in 2010.

'Are You Hung Up?' (Frank Zappa)
This intro track features deep, pitch-altered voices and a parody of hippie dialogue before one of Gary Kellgren's weirdest rants (about erasing all of Frank Zappa's masters) plays. A brief and taut guitar solo plays before Jimmy Carl Black's introduction as 'the Indian of the group.'

'Who Needs the Peace Corps?' (Frank Zappa)
The thesis statement of the album. Zappa composes a straight ode to the hypocrisy of the hippies. The first verse is particularly brutal:

> *I'm completely stoned*
> *I'm hippy and I'm trippy*
> *I'm a gypsy on my own...*
> *I'm really just a phony*
> *But forgive me*
> *'Cause I'm stoned*

The music hinges on a keyboard melody, shuffling acoustic guitar, woodwinds, and a few simple tempo and melody changes. The lyrics mock San Francisco ('every town must have a place where phony hippies meet, psychedelic dungeons popping up on every street.') and more.

'Concentration Moon' (Frank Zappa)
A swell of organ announces the soft waltz with an old-time sing-a-long feel. Acoustic guitar is used prominently to highlight lyrics such as: 'Wish I was back in the alley with all of my friends. Still running free: Hair growing out every

hole in me.' The shift to the 4/4 chorus creates a martial feel as the band sings about police brutality: 'cop kill a creep, pow pow pow!' Though simple in construction, the vocal harmonies are strong.

'Mom and Dad' (Frank Zappa)

Zappa plays it completely straight here, creating a truly beautiful examination of generational conflicts. The mournful melody and arrangement highlight heart-wrenching lyrics such as:

> *Someone said they made some noise*
> *The cops have shot some girls and boys*
> *You'll sit home and drink all night*
> *'They looked too weird ... it served them right'*

In just four lines, Zappa distills the generational conflict that had reached an intensity seldom seen before or since. During the stunning bridge, Zappa throws blame at the parents:

> *Ever take a minute just to show a real emotion*
> *In between the moisture cream and velvet facial lotion?*
> *Ever tell your kids you're glad that they can think?*
> *Ever say you loved 'em? Ever let 'em watch you drink?*
> *Ever wonder why your daughter looked so sad?*
> *It's such a drag to have to love a plastic Mom & Dad*

One of the few Zappa tunes that can draw a tear from the average listener, it is a shame that he didn't try a more sincere approach more often.

'Telephone Conversation' (Frank Zappa)

A brief dialogue interlude that showcases paranoid rambling between Zappa, the operator, and two women named Pam and Vicki, indicative of the increasing anxiety and distrust growing during the Johnson years and, later, the Nixon Administration.

'Bow Tie Daddy' (Frank Zappa)

A brief excursion into pre-war jazz, the lyrics retain the paranoia of the previous track including lines like 'don't try to do no thinking, just go on with your drinking.' Ouch.

'Harry You're a Beast' (Frank Zappa)

This tune is very unpleasant. While the arrangement and melodies remain strong, Zappa bashes the Women's Liberation movement: 'you paint your head, your mind is dead, you don't even know what I just said. That's you. American womanhood!' There is then a lyrical passage implying a rape at the end. Though the man in the song is portrayed as a monster here, this track is hard to listen to in modern times.

'What's the Ugliest Part of Your Body?' (Frank Zappa)
A thankful return to broad social view, the title question is answered bluntly: 'I think it's your mind.' The slow verses slam into a chorus describing one of Frank's life mottoes: 'All your children are poor unfortunate victims of systems beyond their control. A plague upon your ignorance and the gray despair of your ugly life'.

'Absolutely Free' (Frank Zappa)
As the centerpiece of the album, 'Absolutely Free' is a tour-de-force. The piano introduction (gorgeous) leads to Frank defining 'discorporate,' which showcases what Zappa considered the condescending view of youth culture taken by others. The music follows a waltz time and includes pianos, acoustic guitars, and parodic hippie lyrics. The melody and the singing are so spot-on that it would be easy to mistake the song for a real psychedelic anthem:

> *Discorporate and come with me*
> *Shifting, drifting, cloudless, starless*
> *velvet valleys and a sapphire sea*

Zappa then makes his point clear by stating 'flower power sucks' which echoes, loops, and increases in volume and intensity as the lyrics continue:

> *Diamonds on velvets on goldens on vixen*
> *On Comet and Cupid, on Donner and Blitzen*
> *On up and away and afar and a go-go*
> *Escape from the weight of your corporate logo!*

Zappa was dedicated to freedom and love but couldn't stand the corporate takeover of the movement. Two lines, in particular, showcase his true life philosophy: 'Freedom, freedom, kindly loving. You'll be absolutely free, only if you want to be.'

'Flower Punk' (Frank Zappa)
Musically, this song is a variation of the folk standard 'Hey Joe' popularized by Hendrix. However, it focuses on the hippie lifestyle including lines like 'I'm goin' up to Frisco to join a psychedelic band' and 'I'm going to the shrink so he can help me be a nervous wreck.' The vocal layering on the ending is disorienting, including two sped-up Zappas reciting similar, but conflicting, stories in each stereo channel while voices in the center rant wildly.

'Hot Poop' (Frank Zappa)
Kellergren ranting against Zappa and the backward 'Mother People' verse ends the side.

'Nasal Retentive Calliope Music' (Frank Zappa)
Mad noise-making starts side two. Lots of shrieking electronics, and Eric Clapton (allegedly) shouting 'Beautiful! God! It's God, I see God!' before Zappa inserts a failed Studio Z single, 'Heavies,' at the end.

'Let's Make the Water Turn Black' (Frank Zappa)
The hippie-bashing of the first side changes as Zappa waxes nostalgic. The instrumentation here is the simplest on the album. The melody, however, goes through many ups, downs, climaxes, twists, turns, and changes.

'The Idiot Bastard Son' (Frank Zappa)
More social satire continues the story of his two schoolyard friends. Droning guitars and 'snorks' give way to gorgeous flute melodies and biting lyrics like: 'The idiot bastard son: The father's a Nazi in congress today, the mother's a hooker somewhere in LA.' Later lyrics describe Kenny and Ronnie entering the world of 'liars and cheaters and people like you,' a direct shot at the listener: and not his last.

'Lonely Little Girl' (Frank Zappa)
Hard rock examination of how parents don't understand their children. A reprise of 'What's The Ugliest Part of Your Body?' ('all your children are poor unfortunate victims') creates conceptual continuity. And the melody is beautiful: an underrated track I always forget until it's playing.

'Take Your Clothes Off When You Dance' (Frank Zappa)
The lyrical version of a melody from *Lumpy Gravy* features a rock arrangement detailing more Zappa philosophy:

> *There will come a time when everybody*
> *Who is lonely will be free to sing and dance and love*
> *There will come a time when every evil*
> *That we know will be an evil that we can rise above.*
> *Who cares if hair is long or short or sprayed or partly grayed*
> *We know that hair ain't where it's at.*

'What's the Ugliest Part of Your Body?' (Frank Zappa)
This very brief doo-wop reprise mocks the reprises from *Sgt. Peppers*, with a slower tempo that abruptly increases when the tape is sped up to absurdity.

'Mother People' (Frank Zappa)
The penultimate track positions Zappa and the Mothers as 'The Other People' and attempts to explain how perception influences our understanding of others. The music is the catchiest on the album, with particularly excellent drumming, wah guitar, and harmonic vocals. The song ends with an excerpt of 'I Don't Know If I Can Go Through This Again' from *Lumpy Gravy*.

'The Chrome Plated Megaphone of Destiny' (Frank Zappa)
Hardcore avant is explored here, with dissonant piano, shrill woodwinds, random drums, electronic edits, and more coalescing into an arresting piece. Uncomfortable laughs, grunts, and 'snorks' combine with slowed backing music to create one of Frank's best 'difficult' pieces. Varese would have approved.

Cruising with Ruben and the Jets (1968)

Personnel:
Frank Zappa: lead guitar, drums, piano, bass, and vocals
Jimmy Carl Black: drums
Ray Collins: lead vocals
Roy Estrada: electric bass and vocals
Bunk Gardner: tenor and alto sax
Don Preston: keyboards
Motorhead Sherwood: baritone sax and tambourine
Arthur Dyer Tripp III: drums
Ian Underwood: keyboards, tenor, and alto sax
Recorded: December 1967 through February 1968
Released on December 2, 1968
Peak Chart Position: Number 110 on the US Billboard 200
1984 Overdubs:
Jay Anderson: string bass
Arthur Barrow: bass
Chad Wackerman: drums

In a career defined by constant changes, *Cruising With Ruben and the Jets* is perhaps the strangest album in Zappa's career. After a diverse semi-pop debut, a wild sophomore album, a risky piece of music concrete and modern classical, and a hippie-bashing psychedelic suite, Zappa and the Mothers released a straight doo-wop album just in time for the Summer of Love.

While Zappa had written doo-wop on previous albums, it is here that his love of the form reaches a peak. There is no studio trickery, here, no subtle or overt sound experimentation, no snorks, or harsh noises. It is a true tribute to doo-wop and a loving exploration of the form. The album was recorded for the *No Commercial Potential* project and was a concept album. The underlying theme is that a band of anthropomorphic dogs are performing the album under the name Ruben and the Jets. Amusingly, a band did later form under that name to produce two high-quality doo-wop albums produced by Frank.

The origin of the album centered around a discussion engineer Dick Kunc had with the band. They were talking about how much they loved doo-wop, which inspired Ray Collins to start singing a few of their favorites. Collins was increasingly alienated from the rest of the band and was on the verge of leaving the group when Zappa suggested recording the album. Collins stayed long enough to record it before leaving. Collins' lead performances throughout the album are fantastic, and the album is, in many ways, a wonderful tribute to him. Collins had this to say:

> *I brought the style of being raised in Pomona, California, being raised on the Four Aces, the Four Freshmen, Frankie Lane, Frank Sinatra and Jesse Baldwin... Frank actually had more influences from the 'real blues', you*

know, like Muddy Waters, those kind of people. But I wasn't into that in my early life. I was more of the pop culture, pop radio things...

Bunk Gardner stated that *Cruising* was '...an easy album to record. We were recording it at the same time as *Uncle Meat* because the songs were easy and very simple and didn't require a lot of time for arrangements and technical overdubbing.' He also noted that sax player Motorhead Sherwood was enthusiastic and enjoyed playing this material more than difficult and complex music.

To go with the more straight feel of the album, Zappa wrote 'sub-Mongoloid' lyrics to mock love cliches. The music featured a copy-and-paste approach, in which Zappa took a chord progression from one song and contrasted it with parts from another. Zappa also inserted Stravinsky quotes throughout and tweaked the generic chord progressions. The band re-recorded four tunes from *Freak Out!* to fill out the tracklist: 'You Didn't Try to Call Me,' 'I'm Not Satisfied,' 'Anyway the Wind Blows,' and 'How Could I Be Such a Fool.' The ease with which they translate to doo-wop shows how close this form is to Zappa's heart.

Historical note: Zappa's recording contract with MGM and Verve Records expired around this time, which gave them the chance to negotiate – with the help of Herb Cohen – for the creation of Bizarre Productions. The first album released on this new subsidiary was *Cruising With Ruben and the Jets.*

'Cheap Thrills' (Frank Zappa)
The opening track was undoubtedly a huge shock to many. The opening harmonies are fine, and Zappa's lead is memorable. Fun fact: this song is a rare solo Zappa recording: he plays every instrument and sings every vocal line in a throwback to his one-man-band approach at Studio Z. This song could come from a classic 78 single, but for lines like:

Cheap thrills all over the seat
Cheap thrills, your kind of lovin' can't be beat
Cheap thrills up and down my spine

'Love of My Life' (Frank Zappa, Curtis Williams)
Collins' first vocal appearance is a strong one. The echoed production and the double-tracked leads create an authentic sound. Zappa's excellent doo-wop bass leads the way. And the music includes a vocal melody that quotes 'Earth Angel,' the classic doo-wop tune by the Penguins.

'How Could I Be Such a Fool' (Frank Zappa)
The way the band strips down this tune is astonishing. Stripping away the instrumentation layers and focusing solely on doo-wop piano, bass, drums, Collins' falsetto, and vocal harmonies reveals its emotional core. This minimalist approach is typical for the album.

'Deseri' (Ray Collins, Paul Buff)
One of the few songs Zappa recorded that he didn't write, 'Deseri' features Collins' lyrical and musical ideas fleshed out with ex-Studio Z partner Paul Buff. The arrangements feature saxophone, dancing bass, high-pitched Estrada vocals, and acoustic guitar. The music is more straightforward than Zappa's but fine. The lyrics match Zappa's:

> *When I'm dancing with Deseri*
> *All the boys are jealous of me*
> *I'm as happy as I can be*
> *Oh, Deseri*

'I'm Not Satisfied' (Frank Zappa)
Another *Freak Out!* tune stripped to bare essentials and turned into a beautiful doo-wop ode. The differences between the bass and drums of the original and 1984 mixes are pronounced. The echoing production of the original does overshadow some arrangement details but feels authentic to the genre. The tighter and cleaner 1984 performances open up the frequency range and allow the listener to hear the excellent vocal harmonies and piano part. However, the difference in the production styles is very pronounced and can be distracting.

'Jelly Roll Gum Drop' (Frank Zappa)
For whatever reason, I adore this tune for its sense of naivety and simplicity, which feels authentic. The upbeat melodies of the vocals, bass, drums, and guitar are perhaps almost simplistic but remain fun. Sherwood's saxophone interjections add a spicy R&B sound that deepens the tonal range.

'Anything' (Ray Collins)
Collins' biggest musical contribution to the band is this doo-wop gem. The I-IV-V piano progression forms a sturdy if predictable, background for his vocal melodies. The vocal performance here is fantastic – Collins' lead and the harmonies feel engaged with the material in a non-ironic way, and Sherwood's sax solo is among his finest. The band said that playing on and arranging this song was one of the highlights of the session.

'Later That Night' (Frank Zappa, Billy Hill)
Opening side two with more Zappa bass vocals, 'Later That Night' also includes a music quotation from 'Glory of Love' by the Velvetones. The same approach employed throughout the album is executed here quite well. The piano changes are more varied and complex than on other tunes, and the vocal harmonies are tight. The original percussion, including a tambourine, feels authentic. The ending spoken-word section adds the Zappa touch: 'I hold in my hand three letters from the stages of your fine, fine, super-fine career.'

'You Didn't Try to Call Me' (Frank Zappa)
Personally, I don't think that this *Freak Out!* tune translates to doo-wop as easily as the others. That said, Zappa adds some fine acoustic and electric guitar embellishments to create appropriate sonic variation, while Collins puts on one of his finest performances.

Honestly, though, I'm finding it hard to keep these write-ups entertaining, as doo-wop – for all its beauty – is inherently limited, even when tackled by a genius like Zappa. I'll try my best to keep focused!

'Fountain of Love' (Frank Zappa, Ray Collins, Igor Stravinsky)
This song features an obligatory Stravinsky quote, drawing from 'Le Sacre du Printemps.' The minimalist streak is very pronounced here. The piano, bass, drums, and vocal arrangements are stripped to the bone. However, the chord and melody change on the line 'we made a wish' stand out as subtle and effective. The shift to a spoken-word approach is appropriate, considering how often such moments were inserted into doo-wop. Though silly, it beats Elvis' bleating in 'Are You Lonesome Tonight?'

'No. No. No.' (Frank Zappa)
The second of two complete Zappa solo performances is among the most inane songs on the album. The endless 'boppa dooayydoo' harmonies by an overdubbed Zappa drone in the brain over Zappa's slightly sped up lead vocal. The drumming here is a nice change from Black and Tripp's, as Zappa was a solid percussionist. A few great lines are hidden among the background vocals, including:

> *Gave my money all to you-oo*
> *You took my watch and pawned it too*
> *Three gold teeth and one glass eye*
> *You didn't have the nerve to say goodbye*

'Anyway the Wind Blows' (Frank Zappa)
The penultimate track on the album is the last of the rearranged *Freak Out!* tracks. Pulled back to acoustic guitar, bass, and drums, the beautiful melody is even more apparent. Collins sells it even better here than he did on *Freak Out!* and the vocal harmonies are lush throughout.

'Stuff Up the Cracks' (Frank Zappa)
As Zappa often did, he saved the best track for last The chord progressions are the most complex and unpredictable, the vocal melodies move through modes and unexpected moves with aplomb and ease, and the supporting harmonies are great. The instrumentation is also lusher, with piano, guitar, bass, drums, and saxophones supporting startling lyrics like: 'Stuff up the cracks, turn on

the gas, I'm gonna take my life.'

More importantly, this track features the first recorded extended Zappa guitar solo. Past lead parts were interjections, hooks, or breaks that didn't become the sprawling solos he'd showcase in later years. Here, Frank is unleashed for the first time to showcase the pain of the tortured singer. The unexpected wah tone is particularly harsh and contrasts well with the piano. And while it isn't on par with later explorations, it shows he's becoming a high-caliber soloist.

Uncle Meat (1969)

Personnel:
Frank Zappa: guitar, 'low grade' vocals, and percussion)
Ray Collins: 'swell' vocals
Jimmy Carl Black: drums, 'droll humor,' and 'poverty')
Roy Estrada: electric bass, 'cheeseburgers,' and 'Pachuco falsetto')
Don (Dom De Wild) Preston: electric piano, 'tarot cards,' and 'brown rice'
Billy (The Oozer) Mundi drums 'on some pieces before he quit to join RHINOCEROS'
Bunk (Sweetpants) Gardner: piccolo, flute, clarinet, bass clarinet, soprano sax, alto sax, tenor sax, and bassoon (all of these electric and/or non-electric depending)'
Ian Underwood: electric organ, piano, harpsichord, celeste, flute, clarinet, alto sax, baritone sax, 'special assistance,' 'copyist,' 'industrial relations' and 'teen appeal'
Artie (With the Green Mustache) Tripp: drums, timpani, vibes, marimba, xylophone, wood blocks, bells, small chimes, 'cheerful outlook' and 'specific enquiries'
Euclid James (Motorhead/Motorishi) Sherwood: 'pop star,' 'frenetic' tenor sax 'stylings,' tambourine, choreography, 'obstinance' and 'equipment setter-upper when he's not hustling local groupies'
Recorded on October 1967 to February 1968; percussion overdubs, March and April 1968
Percussion Overdubs: March-April, 1968.
Released on April 1969.
Producer: Frank Zappa.
Engineer: Richard 'Dynamite Dick' Kunc.
Peak Chart Position: Number 43 on the US Billboard 200
Guest Musicians:
Pamela Zarubica as Suzy Creamcheese vocals
Ruth Komanoff (later Underwood): marimba and vibes with Artie 'on many of the tracks'
Nelcy Walker: soprano voice on 'Dog Breath' and 'The Uncle Meat Variations.'

The last piece of the *No Commercial Potential* puzzle was the most ambitious. Everything done on earlier albums is explored here in greater depth and adventure. You get percussive pieces, orchestral stabs, 'Louie Louie' on a pipe organ, soprano vocalizations, endless melodic variations, mad improvisation, doo-wop, catchy melodies, smutty humor, angry band arguments recorded, and more over an intense 75 minutes: the longest studio project by the Mothers.

The album was designed as the soundtrack to a bizarre sci-fi horror movie. The idea came from Zappa and Cal Schenkel, the artist who did many of Zappa's early album covers, including *Cruising With Ruben and the Jets*. Schenkel said:

> *I started working on the story of **Ruben and the Jets** that is connected with the **Uncle Meat** story, which is this old guy turns this teenage band into these dog snout people... That came out of my love for comics and that style, the anthropomorphic animals...*

Descriptions of the plot include evil scientists vowing revenge, mystical potions, Mexican slaves, mutant monsters, The Mothers as a rock and roll heroes, dog people, 'I Like Ike,' doo-wop, sock hops, helicopters, and insane vegetables. Clearly the idea – some of which was filmed and later released on a shoddy VHS – was beyond what Frank and the band were capable of creating.

The complications of filming increased as the band worked simultaneously on four different albums and touring to stay financially solvent. The band was struggling to make ends meet, as immortalized in a taped argument between drummer Jimmy Carl Black and Frank featured on this album. The film was eventually abandoned but not before the soundtrack was released to raise funds to finish it. Surprisingly, the soundtrack format fit Zappa's style and let him break outside of the concept approach he had taken previously and explore more in-depth musicality. In his words:

> *(Music fans are) accustomed to accepting everything that was handed to them ... politically, musically, socially – everything. Somebody would just hand it to them, and they wouldn't question it. It was my campaign in those days to do things that would shake people out of that complacency, or that ignorance and make them question things.*

Fans listening to *Uncle Meat* were exposed to a dazzling array of ideas, genres, and approaches in tracks that sometimes barely stretched over two minutes long. Frank wanted to show the world – and his audience – that he was not a gimmick and stretched the limits of his composition style and pushed the Mothers' playing to its max.

Expect anything with this album. Elaborate modern classical miniatures mutate into rock and roll songs that go through melodic variations before a fall into free jazz. Swells of orchestral music surge over complex percussion parts, which required the assistance of Ruth Romanoff (later to marry Ian Underwood), a percussionist who remained with Frank for several years. Five people play percussion: Black, Billy Mundi, Art Tripp III (all on drums), with Zappa and Romanoff playing other percussion parts. Ruth, in particular, plays her trademark fast-paced, melodic, and dazzling vibraphone and marimba well. Longtime members Roy Estrada and Motorhead Sherwood remain solid instrumentalists throughout while Ian Underwood, on saxes and keyboards, plays well off of Buck Gardner.

The finished album was Zappa's second double album in five years with material arranged to create constant contrasts. In spite of the difficulties of the music, the album made it as high as 43 on the album charts. The reviews were glowing: *The New Rolling Stone Album Guide* called it an 'inspired monstrosity' – a positive statement, if you can believe it – while other reviewers praised Zappa's willingness to take risks and explore new sonic approaches.

Fans and critics alike adored the 'King Kong' suite, a jazz fusion piece that is among his many signature tunes. At this point in his career, Zappa had more than lived up to his youthful promise and seemed capable of just about anything.

Historical Note: Early CD releases of *Uncle Meat* expanded the double album considerably by adding 40 minutes of audio from the VHS tape and 'Tengo Na Minchia Tanta,' a track recorded in 1987 with a cretinous Italian journalist named Massimo Bassoli.

These bonus tracks pop up before 'King Kong' and interrupt the original album's flow. And while the movie dialogue is fun to listen to once, 'Tengo Na Minchia Tanta' is completely out of place and may be the worst song Frank ever wrote. Thankfully, the original 1969 mix was restored with the *Meat Light* release of 2016.

'Uncle Meat (Main Title Theme)' (Frank Zappa)
The impact of Ruth is immediately obvious from the very first notes on the album. Her melodic vibraphone dances across a dense percussive bed, including snare blasts from Zappa. The melodies and harmonies remain upbeat, modern, and unpredictable. Variations include swapping scales, such as C, B flat, and multiple A modes. Harmonized fourths are used quite liberally. Versions of 'Uncle Meat' show up on several live albums, including every *Roxy* release, *The Dub Room Special*, and an orchestral version on the superlative *The Yellow Shark*.

'The Voice of Cheese' (Frank Zappa)
The return of Suzy Cream Cheese is paired with snorks, dead-pan narratives, and cursing. Dialogue from the movie, perhaps?

'Nine Types of Industrial Pollution' (Frank Zappa)
This astonishing track is a guitar solo sped up to create a unique tone, with the non-altered version on 'Meat Light' being nearly 10 minutes. The solo, along with the accompanying percussion backing, is a typical Zappa performance of the time, with everything in Bb Dorian, with the scattered notes and upbeat playing creating an unpredictable mood. Zappa likely played every instrument on the track.

'Zolar Czakl' (Frank Zappa)
Deep layers of percussion, woodwinds, and keyboards are electronically treated and arranged in a non-tonal manner. Unpredictable harmony and counterpoint create a complex minute of music that shows the seriousness of Frank's composition method.

'Dog Breath, In the Year of the Plague' (Frank Zappa)
Welcome to doo-wop pop, *Uncle Meat* style! Honking saxophone lines receive harmonic support from nimble acoustic guitar and Zappa's finest doo-wop bass vocals. Ray Collins sings the nostalgic lyrics with opera singer Nelcy Walker providing some unexpected support. Incidental music from *The World's Greatest Sinner* pops up across the various themes. The vocal melody rises and falls and reprises in a sped-up version during the second verse. A sudden drop into difficult 'modern' music ends the piece, focused on Underwood and Gardner's intricate woodwinds.

'The Legend of the Golden Arches' (Frank Zappa)
More woodwinds intone various themes over ostinato bass guitar and clavinet. Ruth plays high counterpoint based on melodies from 'Pound for a Brown,' a piece originally composed as a string quartet in Zappa's teens. That piece (and the related 'Sleeping in a Jar') appear later on the album. Gentle woodwind lines clash with sharp harpsichord notes and difficult time signatures in a modern way. More Suzy Cream Cheese lines: 'The first thing that attracted me to Mothers music was the fact that they played for twenty minutes and everybody was hissing and booing and falling off the dance floor.'

'Louie Louie (At the Royal Albert Hall in London)' (Frank Zappa, Richard Berry)
This live track features Don Preston playing the chords of the immortal 'Louie Louie' on an organ before, as Zappa warns, the amplified instruments completely overshadow him. Underwood then takes a wild saxophone solo before Frank thanks the London Philharmonic Orchestra.

'The Dog Breath Variations' (Frank Zappa)
'The Dog Breath Variations' is an astonishing piece of music. A dizzying array of meters occur sporadically throughout the piece and create an off-kilter feel. Harmonic and melodic changes (including repeated counterpoint) play out over percussion, acoustic guitar, and multiple types of electric keyboards. And, amazingly, you can sing along to it if you try hard enough.

'Sleeping in a Jar' (Frank Zappa)
This brief and gentle tune originated as part two of the aforementioned teenage string quartet. Instrumentation focuses heavily on trumpet, sped-up guitar, and tumbling percussion. The late-night atmosphere here is fascinating and one that Zappa's later complex and difficult 'serious' work very rarely touched – though this later material does achieve unique effects of its own.

'Our Bizarre Relationship' (Frank Zappa)
The lengthiest Suzy Cream Cheese monologue focuses mostly on Zappa's

proficiency with groupies. Only sort of funny.

'The Uncle Meat Variations' (Frank Zappa)
A lengthy exploration of the title theme features tight composing and playing. The initial variation is based on the third section of the theme before flying off into fast-paced harpsichord arpeggios, gorgeous woodwind melodies, and a polyrhythmic feel based on 3/4 and 2/4. A slightly sped-up Nelcy Walker sings over this increasingly complex piece to humanize the overwhelming music. Her vocals are contrasted with harsher Mothers' vocals by a singer that I can't identify. The piece ends with one of the first and sharpest bits of rock guitar soloing on the album.

'Electric Aunt Jemima' (Frank Zappa)
Total pop. Collins' voice is slightly sped up and double-tracked for a Beatles-like touch. The vocal is catchy and the instrumentation appropriately basic. A few electronic tones support absurd, but funny, lyrics:

> *Tried to find a raisin*
> *Brownies in the basin*
> *Monza by the street light*
> *Aunt Jemima all night*
> *Holiday and salad days*
> *And days of mouldy mayonnaise*

'Prelude to King Kong' (Frank Zappa)
A brief sample of the Mothers' magnum opus plays over a 5/16 musical backing with a bass ostinato. Minor variations in the bass create some rhythmic and harmonic variation, with a majority of the musical heavy lifting falling on Underwood and Gardner's saxes.

'God Bless America (Live at the Whisky A Go Go)' (Irving Berling)
It's the Mothers irreverently covering 'God Bless America.' Pretty basic stuff: the main melody is played on a kazoo. At just a minute in length, it probably could have been left off. While there is some excellent percussion work at the very end of the track, it's hardly essential.

'A Pound For A Brown On The Bus' (Frank Zappa)
A variation on 'Legend of the Golden Arches' that fits the key and style of the original string quartet. The tracks are sped up to artificially increase their tonality. Frank's return to earlier melodic pieces – and his skilled variations on these tunes – compares favorably to many classical composers.

'Ian Underwood Whips It Out (Live on Stage in Copenhagen)' (Frank Zappa)

Frank was a huge fan of Ian Underwood and highlights that here. Underwood, a very serious and well-trained musician, was equally impressed by Zappa's composition and arrangement sensibilities and joined the band in the manner discussed in the track's opening monologue. The rest of the track is an extended saxophone solo by Underwood over a performance of 'King Kong.' Though by no means easy listening, Ian acquits himself well and utilizes elements of atonality and dissonance throughout. A fine examination of the talent that Zappa tapped for his next project.

'Mr. Green Genes' (Frank Zappa)

Though most casual Zappa fans likely recognize the instrumental variation, 'Son of Mr. Green Genes' on *Hot Rats*, the original is a worthwhile piece. Collins is at his finest here, intoning the ludicrous lyrics with total commitment. The woodwind doubling the unforgettable melody is a particularly nice touch. The funeral dirge tempo may be hard for some to handle after hearing the upbeat 'Son of Mr. Green Genes' but the droning organ and bashing drums create a sound unlike any other on the album. And the build-up to the vocal crescendo and climax is expertly realized by all performers.

'We Can Shoot You' (Frank Zappa)

This track is a dark horse on the album and in Zappa's catalog. It is another dark, but focused, exploration of atonality. The instrumentation creates no discernible theme, but the flute and keyboard playing create an eerie mood that breaks well with the pretty ending woodwind segment.

'If We'd All Been Living In California' (Frank Zappa)

A taped conversation between Jimmy Carl Black and Zappa showcases the financial conflicts that ultimately tore the band apart. Zappa keeps a calm head with Black decrying the band's inability to achieve financial success. And with a later lawsuit from former members claiming Frank had failed to pay royalty fees for decades, perhaps a bittersweet one for many Zappa fans.

'The Air' (Frank Zappa)

'The Air' showcases Frank's ability to write poignant melodies and his ability to tweak pop conventions. The soft and gentle atmosphere of 'The Air' is similar to 'Sleeping in a Jar' but more extended format. The vocal harmonies would have fit on *Cruising With Ruben and the Jets*. However, the song isn't totally straight, as it is played in a 12/8 meter, a signature that simulates an extended waltz. The lyrics, which have been rather mysterious on the album, remain odd:

The air escaping from your mouth
The hair escaping from your nose
My heart escaping from the scraping
And the shaping of the draping

'Project X' (Frank Zappa)

The gentle acoustic guitar that opens this track always reminds me of the '90s pop song 'Kiss Me' by Sixpence None The Richer. That connection quickly disappears as unison vibraphone and keyboard parts skitter over the top. Expert snare drum work keeps a strong rhythm, as the music jumps from diatonic to atonal moods.

The two-minute ending is driven entirely by atonality, featuring Don Preston going (de)wild with modern synthesizer (or are those organ?) textures. Gardner and Underwood add woodwind and sax harmonies and melodies that explore the outer reaches of Zappa's extended musical imagination: endlessly fascinating.

'Cruising for Burgers' (Frank Zappa)

This tune may seem like a typical piece of Zappa's doo-wop pop. However, there are six different time signatures, including 2/4, 4/8, 12/16, 6/8, 24/32 (!), and 3/4. These meters swap sporadically throughout the constantly changing music. An expanded version on the *Zappa in New York* album better showcased this complexity.

'King Kong' (Frank Zappa)

'King Kong' is the pull-out-all-the-stops piece on *Uncle Meat*, a masterpiece that Frank returned to repeatedly throughout his career and which may be his signature jazz piece. The opening melody is based on a variation between an Eb Dorian scale that implies F. The rising and falling melody is great, but the joy of any 'King Kong' performance is the improvisation. On this version, Don Preston, Motorhead Sherwood, Buck Gardner, and Ian Underwood solo. Whole-band improvisation also occurs, with Roy Estrada and Jimmy Carl Black expertly keeping up the rhythm while Tripp and Mundi add percussion embellishments.

Zappa provides fluid support on clean electric guitar throughout, though his biggest contribution was editing together several performances into a coherent whole. On guitar, he chords and comps beautifully, creates dissonances, and rises chromatically to build tension. Later versions of 'King Kong' may have more technical skill but few match this version's energy and passion.

Hot Rats (1969)

Personnel:
Frank Zappa: guitar, octave bass, and percussion
Ian Underwood: piano, organ, flute, clarinets, and saxes
Captain Beefheart: vocals
Sugarcane Harris: electric violin
Jean-Luc Ponty: electric violin
John Guerin: drums
Paul Humphrey: drums
Ron Selico: drums
Max Bennett: bass
Shuggy Otis: bass
Lowell George: uncredited guitar
Recorded: Between July 18 and August 30, 1969
Released on October 10, 1969
Producer: Frank Zappa
Engineer: Dick Kunc
Peak Chart Position: Number 173 on the US Billboard 200 and nine on the UK charts

Frank's second solo album is – like almost all of his albums – a departure. Gone were the sharp songwriting, the strange lyrics, and the lovely vocals. Beyond one track, this album is entirely instrumental. However, Zappa mostly drops the more difficult elements of *Uncle Meat* – the dissonances, twisting time signatures, and unexpected juxtapositions – to focus on a jazz-based style.

Throughout his career, Frank's love of jazz shows up in jazz-style chord progressions and thematic development. That passion shows up in its clearest – and most accessible – form on this album. Beyond the complex chords of the album, Zappa's jazz love is mirrored in his use of complex, but memorable, melodies backed with dense and unpredictable harmonies, some of the finest of his career. And the playing? Easily the best of his career up to this point, which is amazing considering he accomplishes this with a skeleton crew.

Besides Frank on guitar and percussion – and a few other guests, including an uncredited Lowell George of Little Feat (sic) on rhythm guitar – almost all of the instrumentation is done by Ian Underwood. This love letter to Underwood isn't mere studio trickery but must be considered one of the most virtuosic and compelling one-man performances in rock history. Underwood doesn't just play piano, organ, flute, clarinets, and saxes but densely layers them to create a full-band feel.

Underwood's incredible performance highlights the cleanest and least-cluttered sound of Frank's '60s albums. This increased tonal clarity was due to the use of a 16-track recording studio, which gives Frank the freedom to avoid the sometimes sonically-tricky overdubs of his four- and eight-track days. Before 16-track, overdubs were hard to handle because they couldn't be corrected and tended to eat up the sonic frequencies of the original track. But with 16 tracks at his disposal, Frank could clean up the mix, avoid frequency loss, and fine-tune each track more effectively. This approach met Frank's stated approach – for this album – of creating a 'movie for the mind.'

Another innovation is the use of multi-tracked percussion parts. Frank was among the first producers to mix drums on multiple tracks, utilizing four of the 16 tracks to create a rich and percussive sound. Other breakthroughs included sped-up instrumental tracks, and while Frank had used such tactics before, here they were used to enhance the music rather than disorient the listener. The result was one of Frank's most coherent and accessible album but one that did not sacrifice his desire to innovate.

And the album was inspirational. While jazz rock and jazz fusion weren't uncommon, Frank's work here is among the most focused, creative, and rewarding of all rock-based jazz fusion. While Jeff Beck and a few other rock artists produced quality jazz fusion, none matched Frank's composition and arrangement. And reviews at the time were mostly ecstatic. Rolling Stone reviewer Lester Bangs said:

> *This recording brings together a set of mostly little-known talents that whale the tar out of every other informal 'jam' album released in rock and roll for the past two years. If **Hot Rats** is any indication of where Zappa is headed on his own, we are in for some fiendish rides indeed.*

By contrast, Robert Christgau said 'Doo-doo to you, Frank--when I want movie music I'll listen to 'Wonderwall.' in a 'C' review. Christgau was one of the few Negative Nancies about the album, though, as it attracted many new listeners to Frank who found his early music too crude.

Historical Note: Casual fans who believe that Frank is the lurking character on the cover may be surprised to learn that it is model Christien Frka. Photographer Andee Nathanson had this to say about the cover and Frka as a model:

> *I wanted a mix of comedy and balls. I wanted to say something about the emergence of female power. Christine was a Tim Burton character mixed with a silent film star. The photos from the shoot that day were so good. The combo of me and Christine really worked.*

'Peaches En Regalia' (Frank Zappa)

Frank front-loads the album with one of his best compositions. The shifting layers of guitars, horns, bass, and drums are astonishingly focused and diverse for being provided mostly by two individuals: the only other two players are Ron Selico (drums) and Shuggy Otis (bass).

'Peaches,' in this writer's mind, is one of the most joyous 'happy' songs of all time. Ian's harmonized saxophones at 1:45 play a simple, but infectious, melody that seems to celebrate life and the joy of being alive. It should be no surprise, then, that this track has been released on multiple live albums. According to the site, *Zappa Analysis*, 'Peaches' is one of two songs on the album that has the feel of a classical sonata. The repeated themes at the beginning and end bookend complex, but free, variations of the melodies. Multiple keys, mostly B and B modes, shift throughout.

'Willie the Pimp' (Frank Zappa)
The only track on the album with lyrics and vocals, 'Willie the Pimp' features one of the few Captain Beefheart vocals on a Zappa album. The track is a relatively simple but appealing blues that functions as a solo vehicle for Zappa. However, 'Sugar Cane' Harris gets some red-hot violin licks throughout while John Guerin (drums) and Max Bennett (bass) provide skilled support.

And while the song is a blues, it's a 'perverted' one, as Frank may have said. The melodies Zappa touches include percussive overdubs, multiple guitar lines playing over each other, tempo and time signature changes, and Beefheart bellowing. Zappa's solo is a fine exploration of modalities and melodies. It's not quite at his peak level but cooks in a more traditional style. Throughout, he sticks mostly to 16th notes with some tight triplets and thick chording. Ian is downplayed throughout the track, mostly sticking to barely-audible piano. However, he gets plenty of chances to shine later on the album.

'Son of Mr. Green Genes' (Frank Zappa)
Zappa and Underwood pull out all the stops here. With Paul Humphrey (drums) and Bennett on rhythm, Ian and Frank create thick layers of keyboards and horns and harmonizing on the rolling melody with ease. The main theme is stated once before being layered with a horn-based counter riff that provides more tension during the second statement.

The main melody is one of Frank's most undulating, providing excellent tension before Frank plays another one of his many excellent solos on the album. Unlike 'Willie,' however, there are interjections and melodic variations of the main theme throughout, that break up Frank's soloing and create an unpredictable sound. Even when Frank is soloing heavily at 2:00 into the track, Ian adds keyboard arpeggios that increase the harmonic depth. At points, Ian becomes a one-man horn section playing catchy riffs, interjecting fun asides, and playing off of Zappa like they're the same person. The sheer number of catchy horn riffs in this piece would feed a third-rate funk band's career.

Frank then brings things back home with a repetition of the opening theme, closing with the same chord that ended the original. Though this song may lack the sheer fun energy of 'Peaches' or the manic blues power of 'Willie,' close listeners will likely be left breathless by the skilled playing and variety of musical ideas.

'Little Umbrellas' (Frank Zappa)
The shortest track on *Hot Rats* by no means a slouch – in some ways, it may be

one of the most complex pieces on the album. It starts a second half, which is often not as highly discussed as the flawless first. However, Frank and Ian don't slack off but simply explore slightly different, cerebral approaches.

The track starts out with a mid-tempo bass-and-drum groove colored by Ian's layered saxophone lines. Piano arpeggios liven up the tune before the two themes are started. The first is played twice and lasts for about a minute. The second organ-led theme – which has a stately feel – plays briefly before the solo section.

Perhaps it is misleading to call this a 'solo' section. It has the feel of a collective improvisation, with Ian playing organ and piano parts off himself while varying the initial theme like a pro. Recorders even pop up briefly, an instrument Ian plays quite deftly. The second theme plays with more dissonance before the first theme returns to bring the piece to a gentle close. Dazzling in a more understated way, it may be the most focused Ian Underwood performance on the album.

'The Gumbo Variations' (Frank Zappa)

The longest track on the album, 'The Gumbo Variations' is not an easy track to grasp. Some listeners may write it off as uninspired jamming, but things are never quite as they seem with Frank. The rather relaxed two-bar bass groove is deceptive, as it eventually surges into sustained horn notes with Zappa playing a busy guitar riff throughout. The tension is sustained well as Ian blows through the bluesy changes. An understated organ provides supple support for this groove while Frank sits out. Humphrey and Bennett are particularly great on this track and provide a constantly-shifting rhythmic bed for Ian. However, breaking down all of the twists and turns in this jam would be a maddening (and boring) task for writer and reader alike.

A few music notes: the main progress is a G7-C-G change, a standard bluesy feel that Frank had used in 'Cheap Thrills' and 'No. No. No' on *Cruising With Ruben and the Jets*. This theme subtly shifts keys, including a unique mixture of G Mixolydian and G Dorian generated by flatting the B of the Mixolydian. The structure of the piece, however, is loose and centered on raw playing power. The sustained brilliance by Ian and Zappa falling create a blues-jazz monster that is pure ear candy, with 'Sugar Cane' Harris generating another one of his always breath-taking solos And don't forget Bennett, who provides some groovy bass lines.

'It Must Be a Camel' (Frank Zappa)

The concluding track features tight ensemble work on bass, piano, and percussion. The theme doesn't immediately take flight, but the playing remains tight until the first pause. At this point, Ian adds flute and sax layers that work up to the most fascinating segment of the track and album. From about 1:45 to 2:25, Ian plays some of the densest music Frank ever composed. Keyboards overlap and play in multiple keys, including A Lydian, G# Dorian, G Phygrian,

F Aeolian, and G Dorian. These scales change on each bar with chords extending far beyond normal triads to become as dense as 13th chords. Parallel fourths abound.

While the section stays within waltz time, Frank uses syncopation on various bars for a complex feel. The constant shifts are executed so smoothly that this section becomes nearly modern classical music. At 2:26, an upbeat bass melody opens the track to some of Frank's fastest solos on the album. Ian retreats to a supporting role while the rhythm section adds embellishments. After Frank's initial solo, Ian comes back with clarinet, including harmonized solos backed by chromatic bass and punchy piano. Shockingly heavy guitar cuts through a mix that moves like moons orbiting Jupiter. A brief drum break heralds a return to the textures of the beginning but with some fine Underwood sax bringing the song, and the album, to a very satisfying close.

Burnt Weeny Sandwich (1970)
Personnel:
Frank Zappa: organ, guitar, and vocals
Jimmy Carl Black: percussion, and drums
Roy Estrada: bass, backing vocals, and Pachuco rap on 'WPLJ'
Bunk Gardner: horn, wind
Buzz Gardner: trumpet
Don Preston: bass, piano, and keyboards
Jim Sherwood: guitar, vocals, and wind
Art Tripp: drums and percussion
Ian Underwood: guitar, piano, keyboards, and woodwinds
Producer: Frank Zappa
Engineer: Dick Kunc
Arranger: Frank Zappa
Recorded: On various dates between August 1967 and July 1969
Released on February 9, 1970
Guest Musicians
Janet Ferguson: backing vocals on 'WPLJ'
Billy Mundi: drums (uncredited but may have played on 'Theme from Burnt Weeny Sandwich')
Lowell George: guitar and vocals
John Balkin: bass on 'WPLJ' and string bass on 'Overture to a Holiday in Berlin'
Don 'Sugarcane' Harris: violin on 'The Little House I Used to Live In'

While The Mothers of Invention had proven themselves capable of Frank's increasingly challenging musical ideas, they were unceremoniously disbanded after five years of relentless and – for most of the players – financially unrewarding touring and recording. Zappa gave multiple excuses, including the infamous Duke Ellington story described in *The Real Frank Zappa Book*.

For those who have never read that book or heard this story, Frank stated that he saw Ellington backstage at a concert begging a promoter for a $10 advance. The moment struck him: if the most successful bandleader of all time was broke, what hope did his band have to make it? This story has been discounted by many, including Barry Miles in his Zappa biography. At that point in his career, Ellington was still traveling by train, paying his band members the best wages in the industry, and bringing along three trunks of clothes wherever he went. The idea that he was in such dire financial straights seems unlikely. More likely, Frank was dissatisfied with the playing abilities of the band. Though they'd grown exponentially, Zappa felt limited by their abilities. This unhappiness with the band is understandable given the style of music he would later pursue, but once Zappa told the band of his decision, they were outraged by what they perceived to be a betrayal by an impossible-to-please Frank.

Members like Roy Estrada and Jimmy Carl Black had been with the band from the beginning, had put their heart and soul into making the band a success and were now being abandoned without warning. Other members of the band accused Frank of stealing their ideas – particularly music created during improvisations – and took all of the credit. Frank was later sued by members of the band for failure to pay them royalties after 1969. There are two sides to this argument. Some believe that improvisations based on existing material belong to the individual who wrote the composed music. This argument is common in jazz and explains how a 20-minute composition featuring 15 minutes of improvised solos is credited to one person. The other argument states that the players' unique contributions to the material – including their abilities and limitations – shape the resulting composition so much that co-writing credits are required. I tend to agree with this argument but don't hold a grudge against Zappa and others for following the one-composer industry standard: ultimately, Zappa was the genius here.

After the band broke up, Frank started compiling leftover material – both live and studio-based – to release ten albums of unreleased performances. He ultimately only released two at the time – *Burnt Weeny Sandwich* and *Weasels Ripped My Flesh* – but some material showed up on later *You Can't Do That On Stage Anymore* editions of the *Ahead of Their Time* live album. Regardless, I don't think that *Burnt Weeny Sandwich* gets the proper respect that it deserves. Its mixture of doo-wop, modern composition, gorgeous classical pieces, and lengthy improvisation is some of Frank's (and The Mothers') best work. Its lack of serious lyrics or a unifying concept may hurt it, but as pure music, it's fantastic.

'WPLJ' (Luther McDaniel)
A rare cover by Zappa of a bluesy song recorded by the Four Deuces. It is graced with a straight and respectful rendition. Frank is solid on lead vocals while Janet Ferguson adds a feminine touch to the harmonies. Roy Estrada adds Spanish exhortations at the end, most of which, when translated, are curses and insults. But anyone anticipating another *Cruising With Ruben and the Jets* based on this track is sorely mistaken.

'Igor's Boogie, Phase One' (Frank Zappa)
This short but complex piece features Buzz (trumpet) and Bunk Gardner (woodwinds) alongside Ian Underwood (woodwinds) and Art Tripp III (drums). The music is serious classical music with inspired counterpoint, rapidly changing meters, and an atonal feel based around parallel chords.

'Overture to a Holiday in Berlin' (Frank Zappa)
This gorgeous miniature features a fairly large band. The opening melody is repeated twice on a combination of harmonized acoustic guitar, harpsichord and piano with gentle counterpoint from the sax and woodwinds. This melody initially appeared on Frank's *The World's Greatest Sinner* soundtrack. After the initial repetition of the theme, a sax-led section appears with

dissonant harmonies which shifts back to a variation of the opening theme on saxophone and harpsichord. The shifting tonality of the piece never settles, creating a sense of confused intricacy.

'Theme From Burnt Weeny Sandwich' (Frank Zappa)
This lengthy guitar solo is backed by Don Preston on organ, Roy Estrada on bass, and Jimmy Carl Black on drums. Art Tripp III plays some overdubbed percussion, and there is also a chance that Ruth Romanoff (Underwood) and Billy Mundi perform, but this has never been confirmed. The solo, for those interested, is in D Mixolydian. The chattering percussion and vamping organ keep the track from developing into the pure theatrics common in most guitar solos at the time. And Frank's superior note selection is, as always, spot on.

'Igor's Boogie, Phase Two' (Frank Zappa)
The concentration necessary for this track must have been astonishing. An atonal variation of the first 'Igor's Boogie' features extensive use of hocketing, one of Frank's earliest. For those not familiar with the term, hocketing consists of creating a melody by playing only small portions of it on multiple instruments. For example, on this track, Buzz Gardner plays a few phrases of a melody on the trumpet before Ian Underwood answers on woodwinds. Bunk Gardner then comes in after a few notes on his woodwinds. The approach doesn't have to be as linear as described here but is used to create a random sound that still creates a melody.

'Holiday In Berlin, Full-Blown' (Frank Zappa)
'Holiday in Berin' is an unheralded masterpiece. Underwood and Bunk Gardner reprise the theme from the first track on harmonized woodwinds while Sherwood plays the jazz flourishes that bring in an appealing sleazy feel. Backing these three are Preston on piano, Black and Tripp on drums, Zappa on guitar, and Estrada on bass. At 2:20, all of the musicians but Ian and Tripp stop to play a piano and percussion duet that expands on the gorgeous theme. Zappa then, seamlessly, edits in a live performance at 2:47 that features Preston, Estrada, Black, and Tripp backing him on a lengthy guitar solo, his approach patient and exploratory. Zappa plays primarily in D Lydian for this solo.

'Aybe Sea' (Frank Zappa)
The cute pun title of this track doesn't detract a bit from its gentle beauty. As a duet between Zappa and Underwood, 'Aybe Sea' goes to harmonic and melodic places that the early Mothers rarely touched and which Frank explored sporadically in his career. While the 4/4 rhythm may seem basic, this track abruptly changes keys, including E Mixolydian, C or Eb Lydian, switches to E and C modes, A Mixolydian, and occasional ventures into A Dorian. Movements

from E to C# Minor and A Lydian are also noticeable. In just 2:46, Zappa and Underwood explore a world of music together.

'The Little House I Used to Live In' (Frank Zappa)

The centerpiece of the album is one of the best performances of the original Mothers, edited from several performances. Underwood plays a nearly two-minute atonal piano solo which is unsettling. An abrupt slam into a fun guitar melody builds into a stunning full-band performance that includes Lowell George (guitar), Preston (organ), Buzz Gardner (trumpet), Underwood and Bunk Gardner (woodwinds), Estrada (bass), and Black paired with Tripp (drums). Throughout this section, the initial guitar theme is played by the saxes, implied by piano arpeggios, harmonized on organ and woodwinds, and turned into a nearly operatic climax before winding down to sustained organ, guitar chordings from Frank and Lowell, and horns. At about 3:28, the drums kick into a snare-heavy groove as the melody is again repeated on saxes.

Zappa then seamless starts another heavy solo at 4:18, accompanied only by Tripp's excellent and fast-paced jazz-inspired drumming. The progression is seamless and the solo excellent. At 5:13, 'Sugar Cane' Harris starts a heavy distorted violin solo that adds blues and soul. Estrada and Black groove while Preston adds touches of piano. This eight-minute solo is one of Harris' finest showcases. Preston gets a piano solo and, while not a virtuoso, plays clever lines. He has a way of alternating diatonic blues runs with dissonant modern classical lines that always feels unpredictable. Cane comes back about two minutes later and plays until the 13:35 mark.

Here, a new edit heralds Zappa (guitar), Underwood (harpsichord, woodwinds), both Gardners (trumpet and woodwinds), and Tripp (drums, percussion). The opening starts with harpsichord arpeggios and changes to sustained woodwind over light guitar. The pace then picks up as the melody from 'Aybe Sea' appears on woodwinds and vibraphone. Another edit – perhaps the most abrupt – at 15:00 showcases a rare treat: a Frank Zappa organ solo. The backing consists of just Estrada and Tripp backing Zappa's strange chord-heavy organ solo. Frank sprawls up and down the keyboard, juts at random notes, plays brief melodies, and makes some beautiful noise while his overdubbed guitar plays bits and pieces of the original melody. The solo comes to an abrupt halt at 17:12 as Frank thanks the live audience for attendance.

This little bit of audience manipulation is particularly humorous, as the rest of the track was recorded entirely in the studio while the ending interaction between Zappa and an enraged fan ('You'll hurt your throat, stop it!') were recorded at the Royal Albert Hall in London. The fact that such a lengthy exploration is pieced together from so many sources is a testimony to Frank's editing skills and the united focus of The Mothers.

'Valerie' (Clarence Lewis and Bobby Robinson)

The album comes full circle with a respectful doo-wop cover. This original was a big hit for Jackie & the Starlites, a group renowned for the strange lead vocals of Jackie Rue. His biggest gimmick was breaking into tears during their recording of 'Valerie,' literally getting down on his knees. Zappa's straight version lacks those dramatics but remains melodic and touching.

'Weasels Ripped My Flesh' (1970)

Personnel:
Frank Zappa: lead guitar and vocals
Lowell George: rhythm guitar and vocals
Ian Underwood: woodwinds and keyboards
Jimmy Carl Black: drums
Art Tripp III: drums
Ray Collins: vocals
Roy Estrada: bass and vocals
Bunk Gardner: tenor saxophone
Don 'Sugarcane' Harris: vocals, electric violin
Don Preston: organ, RMI Electra Piano, and electronic effects
Buzz Gardner: trumpet and flugelhorn
Motorhead Sherwood: baritone saxophone and snorks
Recorded: Between December 1967 and August 1969
Released: August 10, 1970
Producer: Frank Zappa
Peak Chart Position: Number 189 on the Billboard 200

The last album released by the original Mothers is a controversial one. A majority of their albums before it had featured some improvisation but mostly composed pieces. By contrast, *Weasels Ripped My Flesh* is full of noisy improvisations inspired by avant-garde and free jazz. Most of the material was taken from live performances across the band's career, which is one of the first times Frank took this approach. However, other tracks are complete studio creations and some mix studio and live material. The result is a constantly-changing collage of noise, melodies, and atonal work that rarely feels in control.

Fans of Zappa's great melodies or insightful lyrics were disappointed by this album when it came out. The lyrics are confined to only a handful of tracks, with most singing being wordless improvisation or random blather. However, Zappa's more aggressive and noisy style was heralded by many, particularly those who attended the Mothers often unpredictable and harsh live shows.

The title and cover match the album contents. The title comes from a story published in the September 1956 issue of *Man's Life*, while the album cover features a man holding a weasel-as-a-razor as it rips flesh from his face. The man grins and says 'Rzzzzz!' in response. Amusingly, this cover has been hailed as both the best and worst album cover of all time.

And the music, which Zappa claims is 80 percent improvisation, features harsh and challenging textures. Grunting atonal four-to-the-floor sections slam against Roy Estrada yodeling for minutes at a time. Beautiful melodies dissolve into horn bleats. Multiple time signatures are played at the same time. This sound is enhanced by Zappa's cut-and-paste editing. Though the music is mostly improvised, Frank's judicious approach to editing creates juxtapositions throughout each track to give the album its jagged flow. Zappa's sole authorship of the songs feels appropriate as, without his production and editing skills, the album would not exist.

Reviewers at the time didn't know what to make of it. *Billboard* called it 'far-out' in an insulting way while *Rolling Stone* claimed it was nothing more than random bits picked up from the editing room floor and stitched together without rhyme or reason. However, later reviews have been more positive. Christgau gave it a B+ while jazz-based publications noted the free-jazz references and approach. And while later releases, including some volumes of *You Can't Do That On Stage Anymore* do showcase a similarly aggressive attack from this band, Zappa's editing ensured that no other Mothers' album approaches its alienating feel. What a way for the original band to go out!

Historical Note: A very, very low-budget movie stole its title from this album. With a free-form plot, household-appliance-based special effects, and insane violence, the B-Movie-loving Zappa was likely a huge fan, if he ever saw it.

'Didja Get Any Onya' (Frank Zappa)

Buzz Gardner's grating trumpet runs bash against Preston's fast-paced keyboard while Black and Tripp bash the rhythm forward on percussion. Estrada is there somewhere amid the constant stop-and-start rhythm. Black and Tripp set up a simple groove over which Sherwood makes more unattractive sax noises. Preston plays dissonant chords, and all sense of tonality and reasonableness disappear. Lowell George then recites a strange set of lyrics in an exaggerated German accent, punctuated by outbursts from the rest of the band. 'Years ago in Germany when I was a very small boy, zere was a lot of people standing around on ze corners asking questions.' Abandon any hope of common sense and restraint.

'Directly From My Heart to You' (Richard Wayne Penniman)

'Directly From My Heart to You' is a beautiful blues cover of a piano-based song by Little Richard. Frank adds thick guitars, pounding drums, organ, and a wonderful vocal and violin performance from 'Sugar Cane' Harris. It's so authentic and respectful that it hurts in a good way.

'Prelude to the Afternoon of a Sexually Aroused Gas Mask' (Frank Zappa, Pyotr Ilyich Tchaikovsky)

After that beautiful blues, we get more intense noise. Sustained organ, echoing guitar lines, and keyboard and horn noises start before Tripp and Black create another snare-heavy pound that eventually completely. Estrada wails with mad laughter and vocal interjections creating a disturbing atmosphere. The vocals get some keyboard backing as Roy grunts and growls. Frank exhorts 'blow your harmonica son!' as more snorks are interrupted by drums and sax for an inconclusive ending.

'Toads of the Short Forest' (Frank Zappa)
A minute of melodic music provides a respite from the noise. This guitar-based melody is based on music Frank wrote for *I Was a Teenage Maltshop*. This gorgeous piece of music is supported by Max Bennett (bass) and John Guerin (drums) of *Hot Rats* fame. The pleasant melody is then rudely interrupted by a live piece from February of 1969. The percussion and keyboards are heavy and polyrhythmic. The horn players make glorious free noise that Ornette Coleman probably would have appreciated. The best moment comes when Frank starts narrating: 'At this very moment on stage we have drummer A playing in 7/8, drummer B playing in 3/4, the bass playing in 3/4, the organ playing in 5/8, the tambourine playing in 3/4, and the alto sax blowing his nose.'

'Get a Little' (Frank Zappa)
A brief quote from Motorhead sets up a typical Zappa guitar solo. Lowell George accompanies Frank on guiro and rhythm guitar while Preston plays an organ drone. Estrada, Black, and Tripp form the rhythmic bass for this sharp solo. Frank mostly plays in E Dorian but plays the G as a minor third on the scale. Zappa then drifts into Mixoyldian at points (a trick he greatly enjoyed) before the solo comes to an abrupt halt with Frank announcing 'we'll be back in a little while.'

'The Eric Dolphy Memorial Barbecue' (Frank Zappa)
This staggeringly complex track is one of the few pieces that was recorded in the studio as a tribute to jazz sax player Eric Dolphy, a musician known for playing multiple instruments (including the bass clarinet) and for a dense, difficult, and dissonant composition style. And that's what the listener gets throughout this track. The track never settles on a tone as layered instrumentation plays detailed and intricate melodies and sub-melodies. Rumbling percussion and horn interjections pop up at random, while Preston plays sneaky 16th-note keyboard parts throughout.

While much of this tune is composed, snatches of improvisation to pay tribute to Dolphy's legacy. The funeral tempo picks up around the 5-minute point when the drums start playing fast, and the horns play bits and pieces of composed and improvised noise. Preston plays a very Pink Floyd-style organ drone while the percussionists and horn players let loose. Is this rock? Not in the slightest, but free jazz fans will love it.

'Dwarf Nebula Processional March & Dwarf Nebula' (Frank Zappa)
This piece dates from the days of *Uncle Meat* and has a very similar tone. Throughout, the musicians explore counterpoint interaction that is unique for Zappa. The tone is fairly acoustic and gentle until a lengthy collage consisting

of tapes speeding and slowing down, washes of electrical sound, and bits of static working create an uncomfortable two minutes of music.

'My Guitar Wants to Kill Your Mama' (Frank Zappa)
Out of nowhere, Frank presents a straight rock song. Thick guitar drives the arrangement while harmonized horns and fast piano arpeggios create an appropriate bed for Zappa's droll lyrics:

> Later I tried to call you
> Your mama told me you weren't there
> She told me don't bother to call again
> Unless I cut off all my hair

After this verse, Frank inserts an atonal horn-based groove that lasts about for about nine seconds before a clarinet plays a heroic melody over an R&B groove. After this brief moment, Zappa plays a tumbling – and rare – acoustic guitar solo. This break lasts from 1:18 to 1:52 and is probably the best part of the whole album.

'Oh No' (Frank Zappa)
Fans of *Lumpy Gravy* will recognize this melody sung by the fantastic Ray Collins. Billy Mundi is featured on drums alongside Black. The twisting melody has already been described in the earlier *Lumpy Gravy* review, though this revision is sharper. The vocal is backed by Zappa playing along on guitar. The new lyrics are a direct reply to John Lennon:

> And in your dreams, you can see yourself
> As a prophet saving the world
> The words from your lips
> I just can't believe you are such a fool

'The Orange County Lumber Truck' (Frank Zappa)
Fans of Zappa's more melodic side likely dug their teeth into this beauty. The excellent melody (and sharp guitar solos) throughout the track play off each other well, with the woodwind and keyboard countermelodies creating a luxuriant piece that feels modern and attractive. The second part of the piece falls into an aggressive mode with simpler, but darker, horn riffs playing over keyboard grooves. Zappa solos on top in a simple 4/4 meter that never changes. All in all, a simple but attractive tune.

'Weasels Ripped My Flesh' (Frank Zappa)
The concluding title track is a harsh burst of organ noise created by Preston pushing all of the keys down at the same time. Initially used as a way of scaring

off aggressive concertgoers, Frank liked the effect so much he used it at various times throughout the Mothers' live career. Its placement here is particularly grating after the more melodic music of the past few tracks. However, there's no better way to end this album.

Chunga's Revenge (1970)
Personnel:
Frank Zappa: guitar, vocals, harpsichord, drums, and percussion
Ian Underwood: organ, guitar, piano, electric piano, alto saxophone, pipe organ, electric alto saxophone with wah-wah pedal, tenor saxophone, and grand piano
Aynsley Dunbar: drums and tambourine
John Guerin: drums
Max Bennett: bass
Jeff Simmons: bass and vocals
George Duke: organ, electric piano, vocal sound effects, and trombone
Howard Kaylan: vocals
Mark Volman: vocals and rhythm guitar
Don 'Sugarcane' Harris: organ
Recorded: July 5, 1969 through August 29, 1970
Released on October 23, 1970
Producer: Frank Zappa
Engineers: Stan Agol, Roy Baker, Dick Kunc, Bruce Margolis
Pea Chart Performance: Number 119 on the Billboard 200

There were many directions that Frank could have taken in 1970. Many fans wanted him to pursue even more 'serious' music. There was also a contingent that wanted Frank to pursue a less difficult direction. Few were probably prepared for the enigma of *Chunga's Revenge*.

Technically Zappa's third solo album, *Chunga's Revenge* is Zappa's least challenging and most straightforward album to date. Even *Cruising With Ruben and the Jets* had the benefit of being surprising. By contrast, this album is a hodgepodge of music ideas, leftovers from previous sessions, and strains of ideas. Reviewers at the time were certainly not thrilled.

Robert Christgau stated, among other things: 'This is definitely not his peak. Zappa plays a lot of guitar, just as his admirers always hope he will, but the overall effect is more Martin Denny than Varese. Also featured are a number of 'dirty' jokes" in a C+ review. Lester Bangs wrote: 'The public may not be quite as ignorant or as debased in its tastes as Zappa possibly thinks, and I suspect a lot of them are going to be even more let down by *Chunga's Revenge* than they were by the last two albums. It doesn't have the long boring solos, but the grab-bag *Weasels* feeling remains.' These harsh reviews contrast with modern praise, with many fans praising the album for the more melodic, catchy, and memorable material after several difficult albums in a row. The fact that many of its songs became live favorites indicates a decent quality. But the album still feels minor compared to past and future works.

Unlike past – and future – albums, which had an idea or a concept, *Chunga's Revenge* feels like it lacks direction and doesn't seem to progress from past albums the way others had done. The 'point' of the album is not obvious and, perhaps, there isn't one at all. However, there is no crime in collecting great songs, particularly when the majority of the material included is memorable and genial.

And well sung, as Zappa adds two of the finest singers of the era – former Turtles singers Mark Volman and Howard Kaylan – to the band. These two – who went by the Phlorescent Leech (or Flo) and Eddie due to contract difficulties – became Frank's singers for several tours and albums. Perhaps the pop background of these two triggered this sudden change.

With Flo and Eddie, though, came an element that some fans resent: a sudden increase in smutty humor. While sex wasn't ignored in the original Mothers band, Flo and Eddie wallow in it with a bluntness that often lacks subtly or – even worse – wit. The two later said that did what they thought Frank would find funny. Though that humor is more reined in here than on later albums, social satire is also not as prominent. Later albums would increase both elements, but fans of Frank's less sexually-explicit work will likely find much to enjoy here. And, in retrospect, *Chunga's Revenge* can be seen as something of a guidepost for most of Frank's later rock albums.

'Transylvania Boogie' (Frank Zappa)
A guitar-based jam features Underwood (organ), Max Bennett (bass), and Aynsley Dunbar (drums) supporting Frank. This piece was originally a composed instrumental featuring more elements, as showcased on the live album *Ahead of Their Time*. Though simple on its surface, Frank plays with gypsy scales, augmented seconds, and A Mixolydian to create a surprising array of sounds and textures.

'Road Ladies' (Frank Zappa)
During the Flo and Eddie era, Zappa's main focus was the *200 Motels* movie. His obvious obsession here, as this album's liner notes, state that the lyrics on the album were a 'preview' of that movie. This blues is the most obvious link to it. It features what would eventually be a standard lineup in the era: Frank, Underwood, Jeff Simmons on bass, George Duke on organ, Aynsley Dunbar on drums, and Flo and Eddie on vocals. The music here stays within the blues formula and includes a fine A Dorian guitar solo from Frank. The lyrics are about groupies. Yup, *200 Motels* all the way.

'Twenty Small Cigars' (Frank Zappa)
'Twenty Small Cigars' is an outtake of *Hot Rats* that is a clear high point of this album. It features Frank on guitar and harpsichord (!); Ian on piano; Max Bennett on bass; and John Guerin on drums. The track's short length doesn't allow for more exploration, but the main theme and the changes in key and harmonies create a fine mood piece.

'The Nancy and Mary Music' (Frank Zappa)
The second version of the Mothers show off their live chops on this

Genius at work in an appealing candid shot of Frank at an instrument he rarely played (*Alamy*).

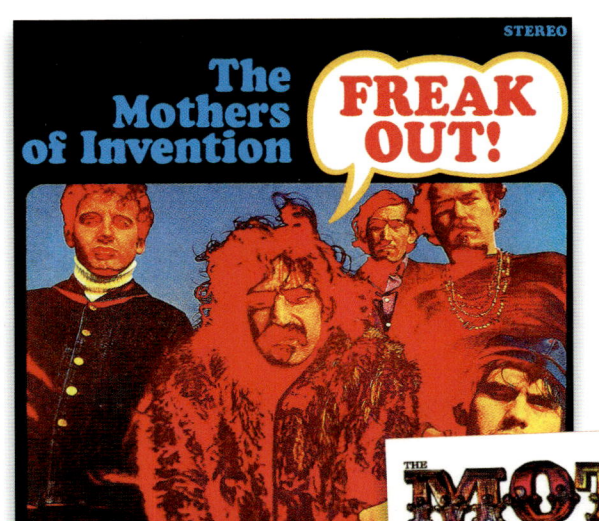

Left: The album that started it all. A masterpiece of clever pop songwriting, arrangement diversity, and experimentation. To some, it's Frank's ultimate masterpiece. To him, it was just another album. (*UMC*)

Right: The difficult follow-up that featured more extended jamming, humor, and a higher influx of classical and jazz influences. (*UMC*)

Left: The first Zappa solo album had a troubled release schedule that saw it go through two wildly different iterations before its final release. The first was a completely orchestral album that was then chopped up into a collage format with rock and spoken-word bits. (*Columbia*)

Right: Frank's finest satirical moment: destroying the burgeoning hippie movement with savage words and beautiful music. (*UMC*)

Left: Perhaps the strangest and least-expected Mothers album, purely due to its normality. A beautiful doo-wop album played with sincerity and perfection. It has a wonderful album cover, too. (*UMC*)

Right: *Uncle Meat,* the movie, may never have come out as intended, but the soundtrack was a startling expansion of Frank's compositional vision and the textures here approach avant classical and jazz more often than rock. (*UMC*)

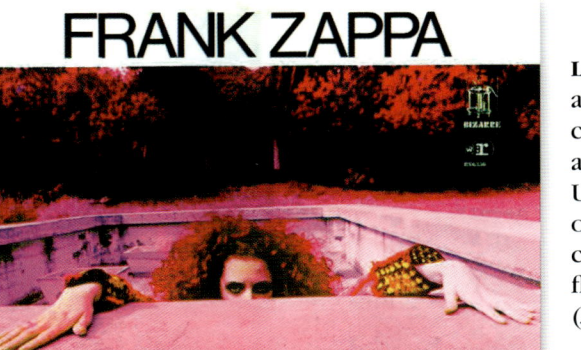

Left: Though billed as a solo album, *Hot Rats* could justifiably be classed as a 'Frank Zappa-Ian Underwood' album. The two overdub like mad to create a colorful, flowing, and nearly flawless album. (*Zappa Records*)

Right: Part one of a proposed ten-album archive series that never got released, *Burnt Weeny Sandwich* is a delight for fans of the original Mothers. (*Zappa Records*)

Left: As the second album of the ten-album series Frank planned after disbanding the original Mothers, *Weasels Ripped My Flesh* is very difficult. (*Zappa Records*)

Right: *Chunga's Revenge*, the third Zappa solo album, unleashes a new band and a new sound. More streamlined and tuneful than the original Mothers, humor and guitar become more important as Frank goes in a more rock-heavy direction. (*UMC*)

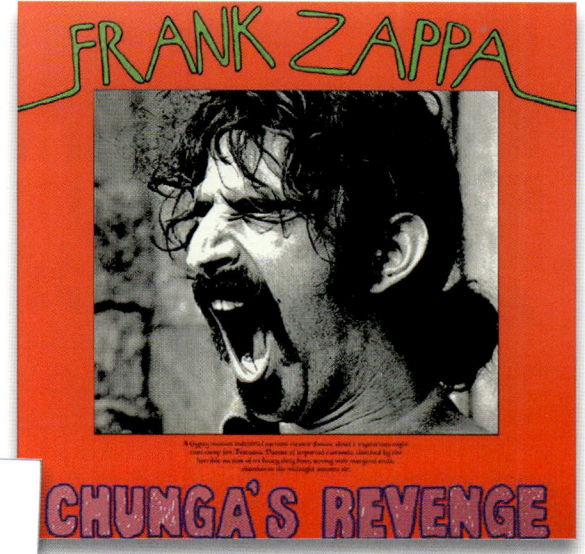

Left: The first Zappa live album features the incredible vocals of Flo and Eddie, a lot of smutty humor, and the sometimes underrated musicianship of players like Aynsley Dunbar on drums and Jim Pons on bass. The Mudshark routine makes its infamous debut here. (*UMC*)

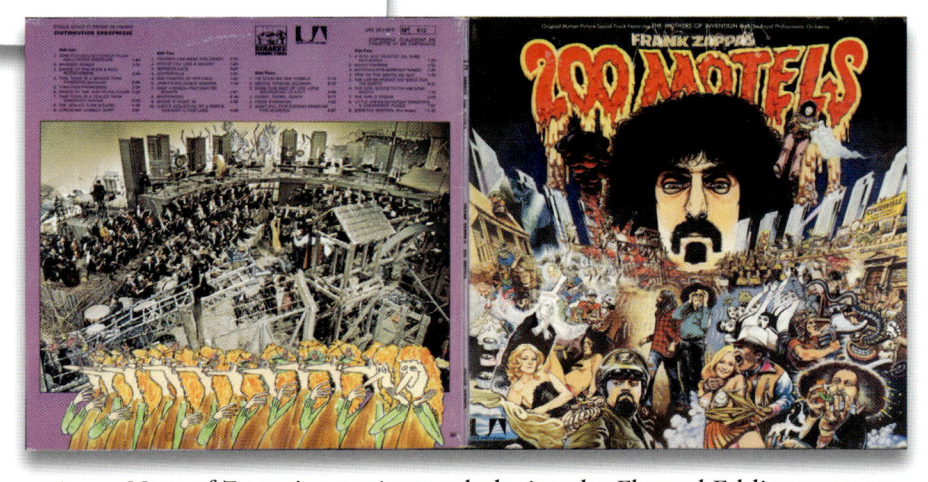

Above: Most of Zappa's creative work during the Flo and Eddie era went towards producing his first official movie release, *200 Motels*, that went on to become a midnight film staple. The soundtrack mixes some of his finest classical music with rock in a successful fusion. (*Rykodisc*)

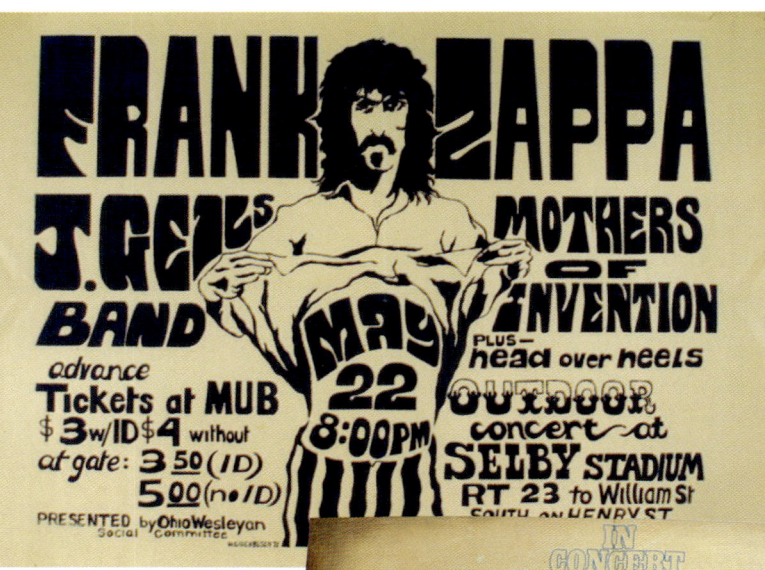

Above: A classic concert flier that featured an interesting drawing of Zappa and a line up that included an early version of the J. Geils Band. The tickets cost as little as $3 if you presented a valid ID! Oh, how times have changed.

Right: A rather beautiful German concert flier that features a lot of interesting graphic design elements, including Zappa, who is framed as some sort of American hero. We can probably get behind that idea.

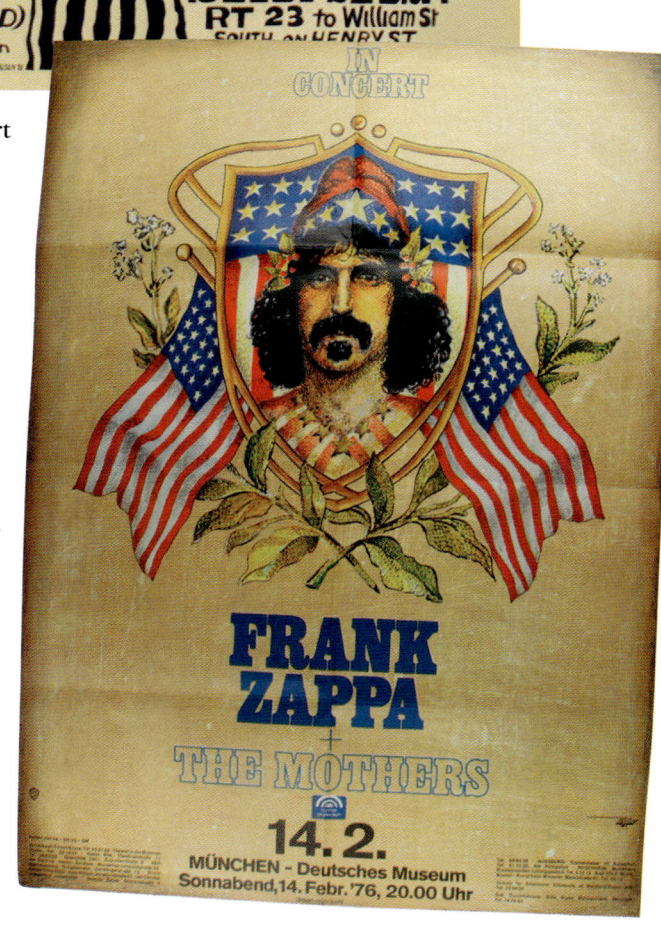

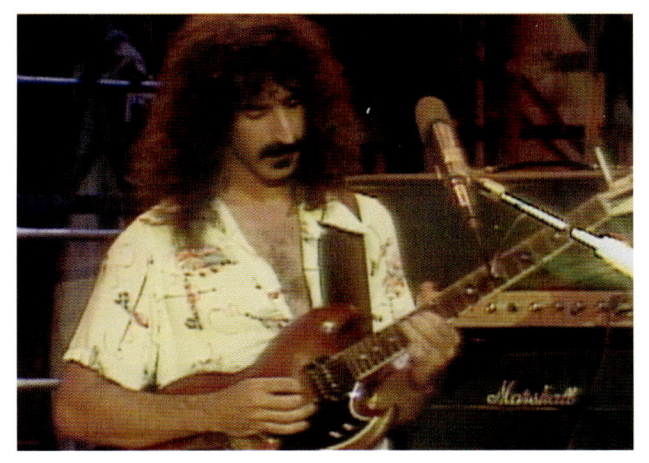

Left: A screen capture of Frank playing guitar during the Roxy era. This fine band was one of his most skilled and diverse, which allowed him to play a broader range of music with more accuracy than ever. (*Eagle Rock*)

Right: A closeup of Frank during his legendary performance of 'I'm the Slime' on *Saturday Night Live*. Zappa was an early fan of the show's initially anarchistic sense of humor.

Left: A shot of Frank circa Halloween 1977 in New York City, playing 'City of Tiny Lights.' Frank's Halloween concerts in NYC were legendary for their rowdiness and fun, and the ZFT has released a handful on CD over the years.

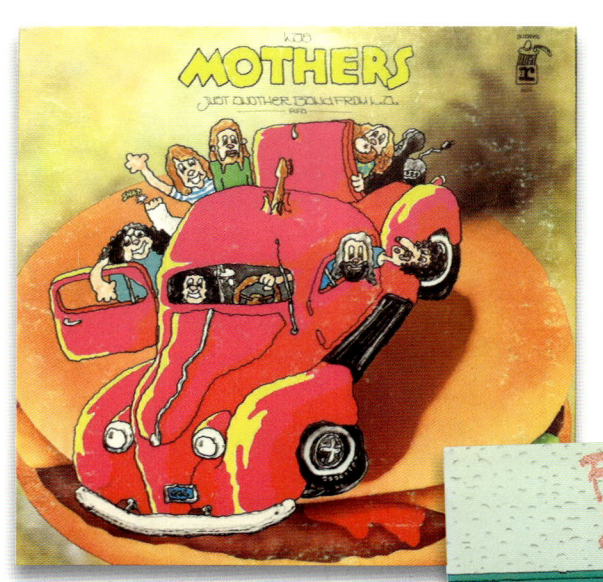

Left: Frank's second live album with the Flo and Eddie lineup features the legendary 'Billy the Mountain' suite and a handful of other tracks that showcase the intricate rock-based abilities of this era at its finest. (*UMC*)

Right: After suffering a debilitating injury that forced him to break up his band, Frank took a 180-degree turn in style and recorded two jazz fusion albums. *Waka/Jawaka*, sometimes considered *Hot Rats 2*, is the most rock-like of these albums. (*Zappa Records*)

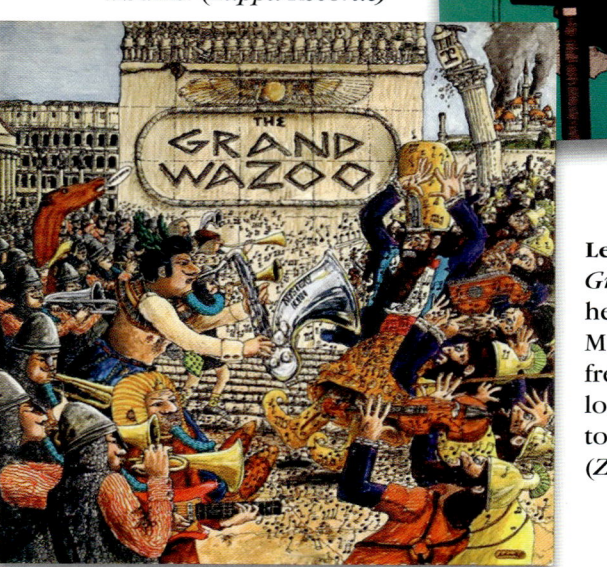

Left: In many ways, *The Grand Wazoo* is Frank's heaviest dip into jazz fusion. Most of the playing is very free, the arrangements are loose, and rock is barely touched upon. (*Zappa Records*)

Right: After experimenting with jazz fusion, Frank took the lessons learned from those albums, added normal rock and pop songs, and created a new style with this album. Although experimentation with sound is mostly gone, the catchy pop melodies and deft arrangements remain a delight. (*UMC*)

Left: The fourth Zappa solo album features tracks recorded at the same time as *Overnite Sensation*, but with a much larger rotating cast of musicians. (*UMC*)

Right: Frank's early 70s fusion of rock and complex musical forms like jazz and classical meet their pinnacle on this classic live album. (*UMC*)

Above: A still from the Roxy movie featuring Chester Thompson (far left, drums), Bruce Fowler (front center, trombone), his brother Tom Fowler (back center, bass and cigar), Napoleon Murphy Brock (direct center, saxophone and vocals), George Duke (back center, keyboards and vocals), and Frank Zappa (far right, guitar and vocals. (*Eagle Rock*)

Left: Napoleon and Bruce get into a tight horn groove. Bruce would twitch sporadically when not playing while Napoleon mugged to humorous effect while singing. (*Eagle Rock*)

Right: The incredible keyboard array of George Duke during the Roxy Movie performances. Duke was a key player in Frank's bands for years and even contributed trombone during the Flo and Eddie era. (*Eagle Rock*)

Above: A shot of Frank's Roxy-era three-person percussion section. From left to right is Ruth Underwood, on tuned percussion, Ralph Humphrey on drums and some tuned percussion, and Chester Thompson, drums. Chester went on to play briefly with Weather Report before being Genesis' long-time touring drummer. (*Eagle Rock*)

Below Left: A smiling Ruth Underwood watches Frank carefully during the Roxy Movie, Her professional career began and ended with Frank, with whom she maintained a tight friendship until his untimely passing. (*Eagle Rock*)
Below Right: The sheet music Frank provided for Ruth's tuned percussion for 'Rollo Interior.' Zappa's scoring here is clean, easy to read, and also features chord notations. (*Eagle Rock)*

Left: An expansion of *Overnite Sensation* with Roxy-level compositions, *One Size Fits All* may be the closest Frank ever came to pure progressive rock. The cover features references to multiple tracks, including 'Sofa,' which is sung from the perspective of a cigar-smoking God.
(*Zappa Records*)

Right: One of the last albums to feature several Roxy-era bandmates, *Bongo Fury,* was the first with drum phenomenon Terry Bozzio. It's also one of the last collaborations between Zappa and Beefheart.
(*Zappa Records*)

Left: *Zoot Allures* is almost totally a Zappa solo album with just Bozzio on drums throughout and a few guest stars. It has a stripped-down approach that creates a very gritty rock album.
(*Zappa Records*)

Right: With a release delayed for almost a year due to concerns with 'inappropriate' content, *Zappa in New York* is one of Zappa's most enjoyable live albums, with additional horn players from the SNL studio band being used to create a dense and often jazz-style sound.(*UMC*)

Left: When Zappa presented *Lather* to Warner Brothers as a four-record album, they balked and started a lengthy legal battle that saw the albums finally released separately with minimal promotion and ugly artwork that Frank hated. Of these albums, *Studio Tan* is one of the best. (*Zappa Records*)

Right: *Sleep Dirt* was Frank's first completely instrumental album and contained more music from the *Lather* project. In 1991, Zappa overdubbed singer Thana Harris on 'Flambay,' 'Spider of Destiny,' and 'Time is Money,' as they were originally part of a never-completed rock opera. The vocals were removed in 2012. (*Zappa Records*)

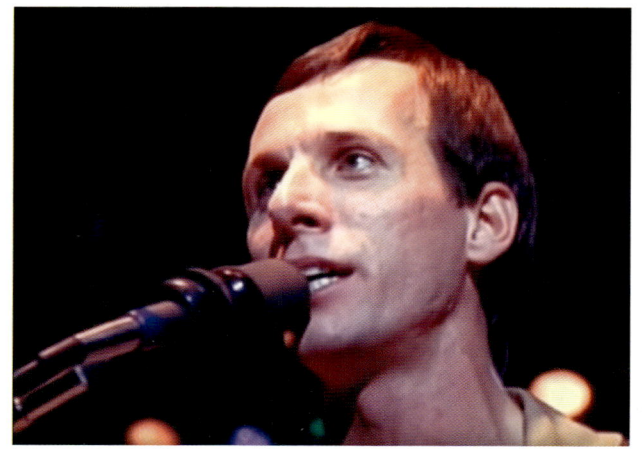

Left: Adrian Belew singing for Zappa during the 1977 Halloween show in NYC. Zappa discovered Belew and when David Bowie sniped Adrian from Zappa during a tour, Frank said 'f&#$ you, Captain Tom' directly to Bowie in reference to the classic 'Space Oddity' track, but with a demotion.

Right: Peter Wolf, one of two keyboard players for Zappa's 1977 band. Wolf was a German-born keyboard wizard who later joined Group 87 with players like Terry Bozzio and Patrick O'Hearn and became a film composer.

Left: Tommy Mars joined Zappa's band in 1977 as keyboardist and synthesizer player and played with Frank on and off until the 1988 tour.

Right: *Sheik Yerbouti* was one of Frank's most successful albums, going to 21 on the US *Billboard* chart. Most of the backing tracks were recorded live at The Hammersmith Odeon in London, and the tracks heavily overdubbed to create a studio feel. The full Hammersmith shows are available from the ZFT. (*UMC*)

Left: The second completely instrumental album released in Zappa's lifetime, *Orchestral Favorites*, was the first to focus entirely on Zappa's orchestral music. A 37-piece orchestra (including rock band) played the pieces live at UCLA, released in August of 2019. (*UMC*)

Right: Zappa's last album of the 1970s, *Joe's Garage*, was a triple-record monster that featured intricate rock jamming, a strange and almost improvised storyline, and a monster drum performance from Vinnie Colaiuta often considered one of the best of all time on a rock album. (*Zappa Records*)

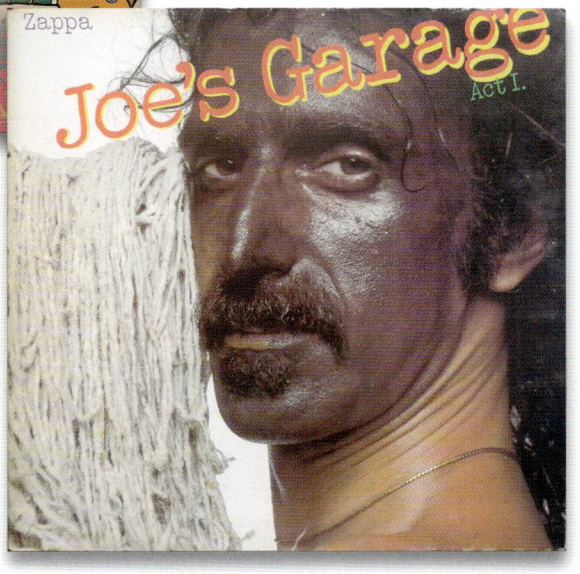

Left: Dweezil Zappa pictured working the studio with an unidentified producer (perhaps Vaultmeister Joe Travers) in the background. Since 2006, Dweezil has taken a rotating cast of musicians on the road as Zappa Plays Zappa, a tribute to his late father, though family disputes have often complicated this task. (*Eagle Rock*)

Right: Dweezil recorded his first single at the age of twelve and toured with Frank in his teens. Dweezil was praised by his father as being a 'virtuoso' when Zappa was asked to rate his own skills, which Frank did not think earned a virtuoso label. (*Eagle Rock*)

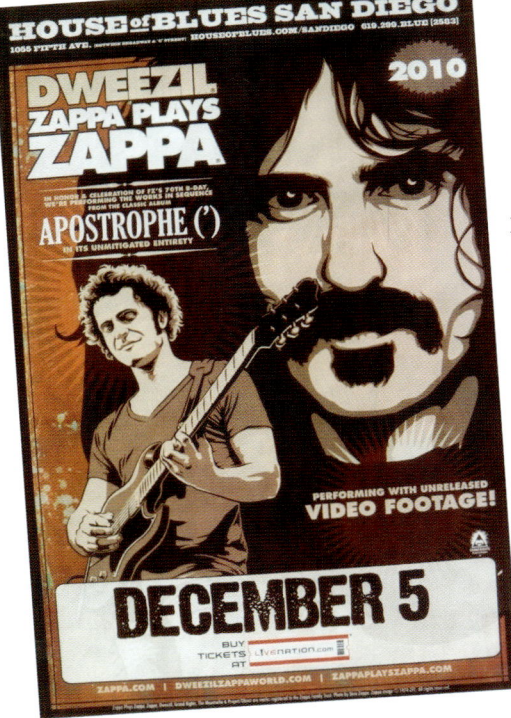

Left: A poster for performances of Zappa Plays Zappa shows that feature a variety of material from throughout Frank's career and which typically feature at least one guest star who played with Frank.

improvisational showcase. The playing is strong, particularly the excellent sax and guitar improvisation around the four-minute mark. Zappa takes most of the earliest solos, including those in Eb and D Dorian. Subtle quotes from pieces such as 'King Kong' and 'Igor's Boogie' pop up from time to time to create a coherent sound. The best moment of the track comes towards the end when George Duke improvises a hilarious scat drum solo. Listening to Duke in this atmosphere – as he would later go on to become a successful jazz fusion artist – is perhaps the funniest part of the whole Flo and Eddie era.

'Tell Me You Love Me' (Frank Zappa)
Though Frank's collection of true pop hits is tiny to the point of being almost nonexistent, the man knew how to write a compact pop song. This track is a perfect example. The catchy opening guitar riff drives forward into multiple themes and variations that all remain catchy. The first 30 seconds of the song contains no less than four different melodic movements, with the main theme getting varied at least two times. The quick speed of the instrumental melodies is a Zappa trademark and one of his most influential. You can see this influence in bands like Cardiacs, who mimed a similar complex-pop sound. The lyrics would be tweaked throughout the years, including on the '88 tour track 'Why Don't You Like Me?' when they would turn into a rather cruel satire of the King of Pop.

'Would You Go All the Way?' (Frank Zappa)
'Would You Go All The Way?' is a great showcase for Flo and Eddie. The two are able to skillfully intertwine their vocals over a constantly changing arrangement. While the melody and the lyrics may be pure pop, Frank varies up the tempo and the instrumental combinations. The first part of the track flows through what can be termed a 'martial' rhythm. The music then changes up to a different tempo and melody as the young girl in the song is approached by a man asking her to a USO dance. Critics of Zappa might consider it sexist, but the point of mockery is not the woman in this case, but the military man attempting to pick her up.

'Chunga's Revenge' (Frank Zappa)
The album's title track is another showcase for Zappa's guitar. This composed piece pops up throughout his career and is found on *Road Vapes, Venue # 3, The Roxy Performances, Roxy by Proxy, Joe's Menage, FZ:OZ, Buffalo*, and *Trance-Fusion*. This early version features Ian on a wah-wah-pedal-enhanced alto sax, Bennet and Dunbar on rhythm, and 'Sugar Cane' Harris on organ. The D Dorian theme is deftly explored, as Zappa cleverly tweaks the feel of the key by changing the melody's starting note to F and G throughout. This change tricks the ear into thinking that the key has changed whereas most of the notes remain the same.

'The Clap' (Frank Zappa)

Another rare purely solo piece by Zappa, 'The Clap' is based entirely on percussion. Zappa plays a drum set, woodblocks, temple blocks, boo-bams, tom-toms, triangles, and much more on this short piece. And while Zappa began his career as a drummer, this is one of the few studio-based instances of his percussive skill.

'Rudy Wants to Buy Yez a Drink' (Frank Zappa)

'Rudy' is a track that budding songwriters should study. The simple chord progression starts in C and includes a C major, A minor, D minor seventh and a G. However, he immediately switches the bass from a C to a D when Flo and Eddie start singing. This harmonizes the chords differently in a subtle manner as Flo and Eddie harmonize in parallels.

While the progression remains the same, Frank tweaks it by playing alternating G and F notes over the top to change the tonality to G Mixolydian. A switch to a 12/8 swing time creates a jarring effect. F Lydian is explored throughout the second theme, while the third theme varies on the first. The brief instrumental interlude plays on a I-II chord progression in C while the remaining track alternates previously-stated themes. All those changes are subtle and hard for the casual listener to detect but add extra harmonic depth to a relatively simple tune.

Note: Duke plays trombone on this track and 'Would You Go All the Way?' and, in fact, received a college degree in performance on this instrument. All the trombone parts you hear on Mothers' albums of this period are by Duke.

'Sharleena' (Frank Zappa)

This ballad is a Zappa standard that has appeared on various recordings in his career. The original hard-rock version clocks in at nearly twelve minutes and graces *The Lost Episodes*. Live versions on *Road Tapes, Venue #3, Carnegie Hall, Playground Psychotics*, and *You Can't Do That On Stage Anymore, Vol. 3* provide fine variations as well. One more studio version appears on *Them or Us*.

Among all these versions, which is the finest? That likely depends on taste. The *Chunga's Revenge* version is the most organic and relaxed. The band play smoothly and with a somewhat funky feel. Unlike the more synthetic *Them or Us version*, 'Sharleena' here feels authentic and legitimately emotional. Thankfully, plenty of choices are available here.

Fillmore East (1971)

Personnel:
Frank Zappa: guitar, dialogue, and vocals
Ian Underwood: woodwinds, keyboards, and vocals
Aynsley Dunbar: drums
Howard Kaylan: lead vocals, and dialogue
Mark Volman: lead vocals, and dialogue
Jim Pons: bass, vocals, and dialogue
Bob Harris: keyboards and vocals
Don Preston: guest mini-Moog solo
Recorded: June 5-6, 1971
Released on August 2, 1971
Producer: Frank Zappa
Engineer: Barry Keene
Peak Chart Position: Number 38 on the Billboard 200

As the first official album credited to The Mothers, it can politely be stated that *Filmore East* doesn't quite live up to that earlier band's reputation. In fact, some argue that this live record may be the worst album released under The Mothers' name or by Frank in general. However, the album does remain popular with certain Zappa fans and was one of his most successful releases at the time. As with any Zappa album, you get some great music, arrangements, and performances. However, the music takes a very heavy backseat to Flo and Eddie, which is both its saving grace and its biggest problem.

Frank said that Flo and Eddie were the best singers he ever employed, so he crafted a mostly improvised comedy routine based on the smutty humor of the former Turtles singers. As a result, many tracks function as vamps or ostinatos over which the band makes jokes. And the main focus of the humor is the infamous 'Mud Shark' story.

According to rock legend, a mud shark captured from the window of Seattle's Edgewater Inn is sexually combined with a groupie. Apparently, members of the Vanilla Fudge, John Bonham of Led Zeppelin, and road manager Richard Cole were involved. Zappa, amused by the alleged depravity, parodied the concept as well as the common rock duty to seduce groupies. The groupies – played by the band members, which is probably the funniest part – want a group that has a 'thing' in the charts, i.e. a hit single with a bullet. The band then breaks out into The Turtles' classic 'Happy Together' to satisfy the groupies. The end result left critics unimpressed.

Robert Christgau stated: 'The usual moderne clichés are packaged with a lot of adolescent sexist drivel from some ex-Turtles, simultaneously dirtier and less obscene than the Fugs.' Modern reviews are mixed but more positive. A three-star review on Allmusic claims 'Whether one considers the results funny and parodic or crass and pandering, the band is undeniably good, especially as showcased on 'Little House I Used to Live In,' 'Willie the Pimp, Pt. 1,' and

'Peaches en Regalia.'' A review in Uncut stated '...their groupie-obsessed shenanigans, and the acquired-taste hysteria of Flo and Eddie, are a bit like watching an aging double act in panto and trying to remember why they were funny in the first place.' Ouch. That said, the musicianship is superlative and moments exist where the whole thing hits all cylinders. Maybe releasing a double album with music outside the groupie routine would have been the better approach.

Historical Note: During one of Zappa's performances at the Filmore East, John Lennon and Yoko Ono performed for a half-hour, mostly improvised set. Lennon later released this performance as the second record on *Some Time in New York City*, mixing out Flo and Eddie as much as possible. Zappa later released the set, with the unaltered mix, on *Playground Psychotics* while taking a stab of his own at Yoko by naming one track 'A Small Eternity With Yoko Ono.'

'Little House I Used to Live In' (Frank Zappa)
This version of the *Burnt Weenie Sandwich* classic is faster and more rock-based. The opening organ chords provide a startling introduction, and the band plays this well – Aynsley Dunbar in particular. With this opening, Frank sets a somewhat deceptive mood that doesn't quite flow with the rest of the album.

'The Mud Shark' (Frank Zappa)
During this lengthy vamp (or as Zappa termed it, 'meltdown') Frank details the story of the mud shark incident to the audience. The band stays on the same chord progression but adds interjections as they react to the story. Get used to that progression: you'll be hearing a lot of it though, to be fair, Frank does warn the audience about this little leitmotif.

'What Kind of Girl Do You Think We Are?' (Frank Zappa)
The groupie theme of the album rears its (ugly?) head on this blues-based tune. The music serves as a backing for Flo and Eddie's admittedly brilliant singing. In this dialogue scene, Flo tries to pick up Eddie-as-a-groupie. The humor of the track depends on how funny the listener thinks lines like 'I get off being junked with a baby octopus and spewed upon with creamed corn.'

'Bwana Dik' (Frank Zappa)
At this point in the story, Howard encourages the groupies on stage by claiming that his 'dick is a monster.' He is the Bwana Dik. The lyrics throughout this track ('my dick is a dagger, I'll force it to fit, my dick is a reamer, baby, to scream up your slit') are cringe-worthy to me but may be funny to many others. As always with Flo and Eddie, appreciation of their humor will vary.

The music here is some of the finest on the album. The first seven bars play a slow version of the *Lumpy Gravy* theme that moves through an E Dorian phrase before the second bar falls from 4/4 to 2/4 to state the second theme. From bars nine to nineteen, another 4/4 section occurs with a C-D-E-F-G progression harmonized in parallel fifths. For two more bars, the band drops into 2/2 and plays a 32nd-note melody that features Flo and Eddie mirroring the tune as close as possible. The rest of the track hinges on a third theme to the very end. This dizzying 2:21 may not be Zappa's composition, but it stands out on the album.

'Latex Solar Beef' (Frank Zappa)
This track title is probably funnier than most of the lyrics and the music is a solid example of the band's skills. The main theme features clever rhythm divisions that are hard to hear but which produce a strange feel. The first theme is in B Dorian with variations in A Dorian to set up the next song.

'Willie the Pimp' (Frank Zappa)
In one of the cleverest moments on the album, Frank transitions from 'Latex Solar Beef' to a slower version of 'Willie the Pimp.' The change between tracks might be the best musical moment here. Zappa skillfully changes the keys to match the next song to create a flowing piece of music. On the original album, 'Willie' transitioned to an ending instrumental called 'Willie the Pimp Part Two.' All CD releases of the album omit it, as Frank believed it flowed better without it.

'Do You Like My New Car?' (Frank Zappa)
The longest track on the album is where the plot comes to a peak. The lengthy vamp focuses on a I-II progress in either F# Major or Mixolydian. Flo and Eddie continue their interaction as pop star and groupie with the rest of the band taking various roles. While your tolerance for this track will vary (personally, I prefer music insider jokes like ' Three unreleased recordings of Crosby, Stills, Nash and Young fighting in the dressing-room of the Fillmore East!' to gags like 'bead jobs'), it is hard not to be impressed by the band's verbal improvisation skills. Though this repeated routine followed a basic idea, the dialogue and jokes were different every performance.

'Happy Together' (Garry Bonner and Alan Gordon)
This excellent pop classic gets a fine (if sarcastic) rendering with Flo and Eddie (who undoubtedly hated the song by this point) attack it with aplomb, rather than crooning it seductively. After finishing, the band takes their leave among much applause, but the album isn't over yet.

'Lonesome Electric Turkey' (Frank Zappa)
Fans bored by the groupie routine receive a nice surprise with this encore

piece. This collage includes Don Preston playing an unhinged Moog solo interrupted by several difficult vocal sections. These abrupt transitions are trademark Zappa.

'Peaches En Regalia' (Frank Zappa)
This version of the *Hot Rats* masterpiece doesn't feature any significant musical changes. Frank was smart enough to know that the track was flawless, and to change it would ruin it. The only alterations include Flo and Eddie singing along to some instrumental melodies. The band is skilled enough – in spite of any complaints I may have regarding the lyrical approach – to pull it off with ease and grace.

'Tears Began to Fall' (Frank Zappa)
'Tears Began to Fall' is a rather upbeat ending for the album and the show, in spite of the ridiculous lyrics detailing 'tears falling on my shirt.' Those who want Frank to continue the tradition of the early Mothers may hate this song, but its singalong nature is contagious.

200 Motels (1971)

Personnel:
Frank Zappa: bass guitar, guitar, drums, producer, and orchestration
George Duke: trombone and keyboards
Ian Underwood: keyboards and woodwinds
Big Jim Sullivan: guitar and orchestration
Martin Lickert: bass guitar
Aynsley Dunbar: drums
Ruth Underwood: percussion
Jimmy Carl Black: vocals
Howard Kaylan: vocals
Jim Pons: voices
Mark Volman: vocals and photography
Theodore Bikel: narrator
Royal Philharmonic Orchestra
Recorded: January 28–February 5, 1971
Released on October 4, 1971
Producer: Frank Zappa
Engineer: Bob Auger
Peak Chart Position: Number 59 on the Billboard Top 200

Fans underwhelmed by *Chunga's Revenge* and *Filmore East* – though each are fine albums in their own right – had good reason to expect that Frank wasn't trying his hardest. Most of his creativity during 1970 and 1971 was focused on writing, filming, and scoring *200 Motels*. As a mixture of orchestral music, rock, electronic experimentation, and fast-paced editing, the soundtrack is a compilation of all that Frank had done before but more orchestral.

The movie is an exploration of how 'touring makes you crazy' and featured the band members playing themselves. Zappa took quotes he'd heard from each member and included it in the script, showcasing the various personalities of the band members. Aware that they weren't actors, getting them to play themselves was about the best he couple hope for in the situation. The film featured plenty of imaginative scenes, great musical performances, difficult editing, and film effects that disorient. The props were obviously very cheap – many were made out of cardboard. Zappa and co-writer and co-director Tony Palmer worked with videotape – the first film ever to do so – to speed up filming and editing. As a result, principal photography was done in five days.

Zappa and Palmer then edited the footage together in a collage that Roger Ebert said '...assaults the mind with everything on hand. When there are moments of relative calm -- say, during the animated sequence, or during the rare moments when only one image is on the screen, we find ourselves actually catching our mental breath. The movie is so unrelentingly high that you even wish for intermissions.' Ebert also said that *200 Motels* was '... a joyous, fanatic, slightly weird experiment in the uses of the color videotape process.' Zappa himself anticipated 'the worst reviews of any film yet,' and the movie was a deft bomb at the box office. However, it has since gained a cult following and was a midnight movie favorite for years.

The soundtrack was, at the time, a financial success but did not receive much critical notice. Rob Houghton of *Rolling Stone* called it '...one of the all-time attempts by a musician and composer to discredit himself.' But in more recent reviews, the soundtrack has been praised. A review in *The Guardian* said that Zappa was a 'far better composer than he was a movie director,' but praised the album as a '...sprawling soundtrack, dissonant and atonal but rich in wit and humour.' *Entertainment Weekly* praised both the film and the soundtrack as 'brilliantly demented.'

Whatever the critical reaction, the soundtrack is the most ambitious piece of music created during the Flo and Eddie period. But, to be fair, Frank didn't do this band much service during its brief career. For example, the posthumous four-disc *Carnegie* release shows a skilled group playing multiple genres and moving through difficult composed sections and improvisations with equal skill.

'Semi-Fraudulent/Direct-From-Hollywood Overture' (Frank Zappa)

Zappa's mocking title aside, this is a great opening. Frank returned to the gorgeous 'Holiday in Berlin' for inspiration, turning that theme into a lusher orchestral bed. There's not much 'modern' here, but it is lovely. Dialogue from the movie includes Theodore Bikel as the narrator/devil and Ringo Starr as Larry the Dwarf as Frank Zappa.

'Mystery Roach' (Frank Zappa)

This straight rock and roll song is designed as a breather between the more serious music. The band sounds fine, as they move through the surprisingly tricky chords and key changes. At the end, the band wonders aloud if they are freaking out singing such silly lyrics: thus, our story begins.

'Dance of the Rock and Roll Interviewers' (Frank Zappa)

This bit of incidental music is a one-minute excerpt of the 11-minute 'What's the Name of Your Group?' The limited budget and time frame made a full recording of this score impossible. The main theme is based on 'Epilogue,' a track performed by the original Mothers and featured on *Ahead of Their Time*.

'This Town Is A Sealed Tuna Sandwich (Prologue)' (Frank Zappa)

The next 10-minutes are a suite of pieces that Frank started in 1968. They are primarily orchestral but feature some rock. Flo and Eddie sing throughout. This brief prologue introduces the basic theme: the town in which the band is playing is a sealed tuna sandwich, which is to say it stinks.

'Tuna Fish Promenade' (Frank Zappa)
This expansion of the prologue features variations on the introduction and new themes for further exploration. Lots of key changes, including D Mixolydian, and tight 16th-note passages highlight this beguiling melody and arrangement.

'Dance Of The Just Plain Folks' (Frank Zappa)
This instrumental features some intricate and atonal writing, some of the most difficult passages on the album. Fans of *Filmore East* are probably bored by tracks like these, but hardcore Zappa fans have been waiting for this type of music for ages.

'This Town Is A Sealed Tuna Sandwich (Reprise)' (Frank Zappa)
The same music as the prologue but with tweaks to the harmony and melody. The reprise is in a higher key to create a sense of progression and movement through the suite.

'The Sealed Tuna Bolero' (Frank Zappa)
The main melodies of the prologue and promenade are reprised here in a bolero. The lyrics continue the main argument – all towns on a tour end up being exactly the same – and include a reference to Jimmy Carl Black, which sets the listener up for the next track.

'Lonesome Cowboy Burt' (Frank Zappa)
This country and western track heralds the return of Jimmy Carl Black. Black is the main comedic highlight throughout the film, putting in the most animated performance and providing the funniest lines ('What's wrong with Sunday?! I smell a commie rat!')

'Touring Can Make You Crazy' (Frank Zappa)
More difficult atonal music that creates an off-putting atmosphere. The tension achieved throughout this piece, and others like it on the album show Frank operating at his finest as a classical composer. Successful atonal music is very hard to write – there's more to it than just ignoring tonal centers, and Zappa is one of the best at operating in this medium.

'Would You Like a Snack?' (Frank Zappa)
More orchestral music combined with a little rock and choral singing. Fast-paced segments collapse into near silence and stasis. As a listening experience, it works well outside of the movie.

'Redneck Eats' (Frank Zappa)
This tune is a strange combination of orchestra, chorus, and Jimmy Carl

Black. Black responds to the orchestral music with confusion while the chorus laughs at his confusion, and the orchestra creates tension. This is another fine moment that highlights Black's comedic timing.

'Centerville' (Frank Zappa)
The 'Centerville' sequence is one of the highlights of the film and album. It features Flo and Eddie wandering through a typical tour town discussing reasons why it's a 'real nice place to raise your kids up,' including its combination of churches and liquor stores. The psychedelic visuals pair nicely with the disorienting string writing: Frank successfully creates a dreamlike feel.

'She Painted Up Her Face' (Frank Zappa)
As one of the many Flo and Eddie highlights, listeners really get a feel for their raw talent here. Instead of comical or rock singing, they sing here in a purer choral style. The music includes rock backing from The Mothers that has a slight operatic or classical feel years before Queen fused these approaches.

'Janet's Big Dance Number' (Frank Zappa)
Many scenes in the film forego dialogue and feature choreographed dancing and ballet movements. 'Janet's Big Dance Number' scores one of these movements and starts a lengthy sequence of mostly classical bits that supported Janet Ferguson – a member of Frank's inner circle for years – as she performs a rather bizarre dance sequence.

'Half A Dozen Provocative Squats' (Frank Zappa)
The band comes back for a return of various themes from 'She Painted Up Her Face' and a further exploration of the groupie lyrical theme. Frank varies the music by shifting to G Major and F Lydian scales. Janet is getting ready for a night out as Flo and Eddie sing lines like 'shoots a deodorant spray up her twat.' Ha. Ha.

'Mysterioso' (Frank Zappa)
This sedate piece features plenty of glissando string chords at slight volumes. This brief interlude creates a mood that matches the track title quite well. Though not a major piece of writing, one can marvel at how much Frank varies his string writing throughout the album.

'Shove It Right In' (Frank Zappa)
The melody of 'She Painted Up Her Face' returns in an orchestral format. The combination of ideas occurs in a collage-like fashion as the chorus intones varying dirty lyrics that are hard to make out but funny to hear a chorus sing. Combining low- and high-culture like this was one of Frank's best gags.

'Lucy's Seduction of a Bored Violinist and Postlude' (Frank Zappa)
In the film, this track accompanies some wild moments, including dancing lizards and much more. These visuals don't detract from the diatonic exploration of 'burglar music,' a technique Frank developed in which loops of various music play at the same time and sync up only at specific moments.

'I'm Stealing The Towels' (Frank Zappa)
The first 10 minutes of the second album are devoted to the wild cartoon segment that is the major highlight of the film. Directed by Charles Swenson, this segment features Jeff Simmons, then bassist of the group, quitting the band to form his own 'heavy' group. This orchestral introduction is just the beginning of the madness.

'Dental Hygiene Dilemma' (Frank Zappa)
The music in this track is mostly incidental backing that reacts to Simmons' crisis of conscious, in which Donovan plays his good half and the devil his bad. The devil persuades Jeff to quit (in a moment that features an abruptly and awkwardly overdubbed Flo and Eddie speaking lines that weren't in the original movie) and steals the room as he goes. Some of the best lines of the movie are in this segment, including:

> *Ahmet Ertegun used this towel as a bathmat six weeks ago at a rancid motel in Orlando, Florida, with the highest MILDEW rating of any commercial lodging facility within the territorial limits of the United States, naturally excluding tropical possessions.*

'Does This Kind Of Life Look Interesting To You?' (Frank Zappa)
Concluding the animated segment is this sped-up vocal track featuring the band describing the average life of the rock and roll star. The acapella style is backed with slight orchestra and chorus backing until the *200 Motels* theme pops up to bring a halt to what may be the climax of the film in general.

'Daddy, Daddy, Daddy' (Frank Zappa)
With a typical Zappa-style breakneck juxtaposition, we land back in the world of pop. Those who've heard *Filmore East* will recognize the lyrical theme (seducing girls, of course) and a return of some 'Bwana Dik' musical elements. Frank mixes in a handful of Mixolydian scales to keep things interesting.

'Penis Dimension' (Frank Zappa)
It's easy to imagine Frank writing this bit of serious orchestral and chorus music and titling it 'Penis Dimension' with a silly grin on his face. Flo and

Eddie pop up throughout and sound great. The spoken word segments focus on the size of the penis and the breasts of women. Contrasted with the classy music, the effect is humorous.

'What Will This Evening Bring Me This Morning?' (Frank Zappa)

Another pop song focused on the life of the rock star, this composition is interesting because it provides one of Frank's few instances of writing in a fugue and canon format. Though the form is mostly implied, it does provide this track with a little more interest than the average pop song.

'A Nun Suit Painted On Some Old Boxes' (Frank Zappa)

A rare example of Frank writing strictly for a choir. This atonal track features soloist Phyllis Bryn-Julson describing 'what gets her off.' The ending line of 'wanna watch a dental hygiene movie?' appears before the cartoon in the film, showing how the soundtrack has juggled the tracks.

'Magic Fingers' (Frank Zappa)

One of the finest pure rock songs in the Flo and Eddie era, this simple track features excellent guitar work and spirited vocals from Flo and Eddie. The music features at least three themes and a guitar solo in A Dorian. Howard Kaylan ends things with a lengthy (and dirty) rant.

'Motorhead's Midnight Ranch' (Frank Zappa)

Starting here, the rest of the album is orchestral and choral. This brief introduction is a typical (but strong) piece of Zappa classical music. It features harsh dynamics, changes in harmonics, and tempo swings.

'Dew On The Newts We Got' (Frank Zappa)

This minute-long choral piece features simple string backing, bursts of 16th notes, and absurd lyrics. The scene it scores is too ridiculous (and entertaining) to discuss in depth here: readers who have yet to see *200 Motels* should give it at least one watch.

'The Lad Searches The Night For His Newts' (Frank Zappa)

After the chorus states the title, handclaps, stomps, and what sounds like someone impersonating a kazoo heralds another burst of classical atonal dissonance.

'The Girl Wants To Fix Him Some Broth' (Frank Zappa)

The chorus is lucky enough to sing lyrics like 'tinsel cock' 'would you like some broth?' and 'spoiled oats in it,' that overlap at various times. The music responds to their vocalizations, including various bits of piano, string swells, and horn climaxes.

'The Girl's Dream' (Frank Zappa)
Very brief orchestral music features lengthy sustained notes and harp sounds over the top of dissonant strings very gradually changing the harmony. The girl's dream must be quite disturbing, as the chorus breaks in to make sure they get a chance to say something.

'Little Green Scratchy Sweaters & Corduroy Ponce' (Frank Zappa)
The chorus takes the lead here, with lots of fine harmonizing and excellent singing. The lyrics mention 'munchkin Irish Catholic victims,' as Bryn-Julson is lucky enough to sing 'munchkins get me hot.' I wonder if she put *200 Motels* on her resume?

'Strictly Genteel (The Finale)' (Frank Zappa)
Frank ends things in a 'sentimental' way with this great piece of writing. The main melody is sung by actor Theodore Bikel quite well: not surprising from the big star of *Fiddler on the Roof*. The lyrics mention various cliches, such as 'rednecks and flatfoot policemen' as the track progresses. The way it builds by adding subtle ornamentation to the main melody is inspired and typical of Frank's style. The song then turns into a rock and roll finale to remind the listener that Frank knows where his bread is buttered. More 'serious' versions of this composition appear on *London Symphony Orchestra Volume II* and *Orchestral Favorites* and on the live albums *Chicago '78, You Can't Do That On Stage Anymore Volume 6*, and *Make a Jazz Noise Here*.

Just Another Band From L.A. (1971)
Personnel:
Frank Zappa: guitar, vocals
Don Preston: keyboards
Ian Underwood: woodwinds, keyboards, vocals
Aynsley Dunbar: drums
Howard Kaylan: lead vocals
Mark Volman: lead vocals
Jim Pons: bass guitar, vocals
Recorded: August 7, 1971
Released on March 26, 1972
Producer: Frank Zappa
Engineer: Barry Keene
Peak Chart Position: Number 85 on the Billboard Top 200

Though this album charted lower than the previous two albums, it is, in many ways, the definitive statement by the Flo and Eddie band released during Frank's lifetime. Recorded live on August 7 at Pauley Pavilion on the campus of UCLA in Los Angeles, it contains some of the finest music from this era of the band. Importantly, it lacks the lengthy – and less interesting – groupie suite from the Fillmore album and focuses more on the absurdist element of Zappa's humor. Most of the album is taken up by the monster 'Billy the Mountain' composition, the first of two 20-minute-long suites of music dedicated to telling a ridiculous – though funny and satirical – story. Both of these suites are complex and unique in his catalog.

The remaining four tracks – which fill up side two of the original album – range in length from eight minutes to three. Two are re-arranged versions of earlier Mother tracks, and the other two are songs with no studio version. And while the posthumous Carnegie show includes more material and – arguably – finer playing, *Just Another Band From L.A.* remains an impressive and engaging listen. If *200 Motels* showed the band at their finest in the studio, this album showcases their excellence as live musicians. One wishes that Frank would have shown their skills off more with earlier albums and maybe cut back a little on the humor. But oh well: a man's got to make money, and the humor definitely put butts in the seats.

The original album was supposed to be a double, with parts of the second record being taken up by more parts of 'Billy the Mountain,' a solo section called 'Studebaker Hoch' and another track entitled 'The Subcutaneous Peril.' The latter track would eventually be released on the *Finer Moments* compilation in 2012, though that version is edited down from the original.

This promise was ultimately cut short during a live show on December 10, 1971. Zappa was playing the Rainbow Theatre in London and was playing an extended encore that included 'I Want to Hold Your Hand' by the Beatles. Suddenly an angry fan named Trevor Charles Howell took to the stage and pushed Frank off of the stage and into the orchestra pit. The fall ended on a hard concrete floor and left Zappa in a terrible state. He later said of the incident:

> *The band thought I was dead. My head was over on my shoulder, and my neck was bent like it was broken. I had a gash in my chin, a hole in the back of my head, a broken rib, and a fractured leg. One arm was paralyzed.*

Howell was caught by the audience and later admitted he had pushed Frank because he thought Zappa was hitting on his girlfriend in the audience. The severity of Frank's injuries forced the band to cancel the rest of their performances and left Frank in a wheelchair for a year with a crushed larynx that permanently deepened his voice. But Zappa, working out of the wheelchair in the studio, took the opportunity to expand from *Hot Rats* with two unexpected jazz-fusion albums that represent some of his finest writing of the period.

'Billy the Mountain' (Frank Zappa, Paul Anka, Johnny Carson, Stephen Stills)

The first side is taken up by the 25-minute 'Billy the Mountain' which is one of the shorter versions available. The *Playground Psychotics* version is several minutes longer and other performances reach almost 45 minutes. Zappa's edit of this performance removed many solos. The songwriting credits include the use of the Johnny Carson theme and elements of 'Suite Judy Blue Eyes' by Crosby, Stills, Nash, and Young.

The best way to describe this track is as a series of 'skits' connected by leitmotifs ala Wagner. The main theme is stated on vocals by Flo and Eddie in the introduction before a simple ostinato begins. Over this backing, Flo and Eddie narrate the story. After this point, various melodies and sub-sections playing, including narration about Billy receiving his royalty check, deciding to go on vacation with his wife Ethel, destroying various pieces of real estate, and narration from a right-wing reporter speculating that Billy and Ethel are communists and coven witches. As Billy and Ethel accidentally destroy various government facilities – inspiring Jerry Lewis to host a telethon – the hero Studebacher Hoch appears. Flo and Eddie state that he looks like legendary conductor Zubin Mehta and make ridiculous claims, including that he can fly, swim, and sing like Neil Sedaka.

Clearly, the song is an obvious satire on the many rock concept albums of the time. Ironically, Frank utilizes more complex and rich music to mock prog-rock than most bands in that genre were writing. The funniest moment comes when Zappa declares that Studebacher can 'write the Lord's Prayer on the head of a pin,' after which the band launches into 'Suite Judy Blue Eyes.'

Breaking down all of the great moments in this track would take a whole chapter. This is undoubtedly not just the signature track of the Flo and Eddie era but their best work. Though other versions of 'Billy' may be longer, this more concentrated version does the same job with minimal boredom. The excellence of this track often overshadows the rest of the fine tracks on the album, a problem common with sidelong suites. Think of how much the track 'Tarkus' by ELP towers over the rest of the songs on that album or how most listeners prefer '2112' by Rush to the second side.

'Call Any Vegetable' (Frank Zappa)
'Call Any Vegetable' increases the element of rock in the original track by adding thicker guitar and organ. The song is slowed to create a smoother feel. Moments of syncopation occur here and there throughout this arrangement, including a long string of eighth and sixteenth notes towards the end of each verse. This slower pace allows Flo and Eddie to emphasize their singing in a way that wasn't present on the original. Don Preston (taking over from George Duke) plays excellent electric piano solos and comps the rhythm in various subsections. This helps to bring a little diversity to a lengthy track.

At about 3:20, Preston and Dunbar begin a high-speed sixteenth-note run that was present on the original and which initially ended the track. This burst of notes is broken up by heavy Zappa guitar which explodes into a trademark solo. Frank sculpts the air with the finesse of a virtuoso for about 45 seconds before the track falls into a call-and-response session. During this stretch, the music keeps a simple keyboard, bass, and drum vamp. Flo and Eddie ask and answer various silly questions such as 'Where can I go to get my poodle shaved? Where can I go to get my stomach pumped?'

'Eddie, Are You Kidding?' (Frank Zappa, John Seiter, Mark Volman, Howard Kaylan)
'Eddie Are You Kidding?' is the simplest and shortest track here, a Zappa pop song with a 2/4 beat, fine vocals from Flo and Eddie, and silly vocals making fun of Edward Nalbandian, the owner of Zachary All Clothing. Edward, or 'Eddie' as he was known, became infamous for his commercials, in which he made many unbelievable claims. For example, he stated that he could fit a 'portly' man into a $30 suit. The title of this track came directly from one of his commercials, in which he said 'My friends all ask me, 'Eddie, are you kidding?' And I tell them no, my friend, I am not kidding.' As a result, this track, unlike Zappa's better satirical moments, is so tied to a singular time that it's hard for modern listeners to get the joke.

However, the music maintains Zappa's tradition of writing pop songs so catchy that they were impossible to ignore. Flo and Eddie do a great job of making the scenario more entertaining, including mentioning legendarily thin model Twiggy. As a change of pace on a sometimes complex album, 'Eddie' is great but is not one of Zappa's finest accomplishments.

'Magdalena' (Frank Zappa, Howard Kaylan)

Modern Zappa fans with little patience for Flo and Eddie are likely appalled by this track. Its references to incest likely feel sexist and disturbing. However, it is important to take a closer look at the lyrics and understand that the threatened incest never occurs and that the girl is never made fun of in the song in the same way as her father. For example, the daughter tells her father to 'go eat shit' before running away. The song then ends with lengthy pleading from Kaylan, describing all the things he would like to do to his daughter. And none of them happen in the song. Does this mean the song itself isn't a little disturbing and off-putting? Of course not. In modern times, such humor simply doesn't fly, and a fan's tolerance of it will vary depending on their taste. Jokes about incest and sexual assault are no longer tolerated for good reason. In this case, however, it is the man who is the source of Zappa's scorn. This doesn't necessarily excuse the song but does make the situation more complex and difficult to sort out.

The music is engaging, featuring vaudevillian elements, upbeat pop played in 6/4 time signatures, 12/8 popping up from time to time, and a lengthy – and impressive – soul parody in which Kaylan and Volman give it their all and commit totally to the lyrics and the music. This doesn't necessarily negate the disturbing elements but makes the piece work in spite of itself.

'Dog Breath' (Frank Zappa)

The album ends with a fine version of 'Dog Breath' that slows the tempo down a bit to give Flo and Eddie time to dig into the vocals. Do they do it better than Ray Collins? That depends on your taste, but there is no denying that they more than do the track justice. The differences, beyond the slower tempo, are mostly minor. At various points, the two don't sing in unison, with Volman singing a slower variation of the melody that creates a little melodic counterpoint. A nice coda starting at 1:29 features a solid guitar solo on top of chromatic bass lines. Fans of the original may miss the doo-wop feel, but this is a great way to end the album.

Waka/Jawaka (1972)

Personnel:
Frank Zappa: guitar, percussion, electric bed springs, uncredited vocals
Sal Marquez: trumpets, vocals, chimes, flugelhorn
Erroneous (Alex Dmochowski): electric bass, vocals, fuzz bass
Aynsley Dunbar: drums, washboard, tambourine
Tony Duran: slide guitar, vocals
George Duke: ring-modulated & echoplexed electric piano, tack piano
Mike Altschul: baritone saxophone, piccolo, bass flute, bass clarinet, tenor sax
Kris Peterson: vocals
Joel Peskin: tenor sax
Jeff Simmons: Hawaiian guitar, vocals
Sneaky Pete Kleinow: pedal steel guitar solo
Janet Ferguson: vocals
Don Preston: piano, Minimoog
Billy Byers: trombone, baritone horn
Ken Shroyer: trombone, baritone horn
Recorded Between April 17 and 21 and various dates in May, 1972
Released: July 5, 1972
Producer: Frank Zappa
Engineers: Marshall Brevitz, Kerry McNabb
Peak Chart Position: Number 152 on the Billboard Top 200

During early 1972, while Frank was still recovering from his injuries, he gathered a huge band to record his fourth solo album, *Waka/Jawaka*. It would be an expansion on the jazz-fusion of *Hot Rats*. In fact, the album is often called *Waka/Jawaka – Hot Rats* due to the cover.

However, this record and its sister album *The Grand Wazoo* are different from *Hot Rats* for a variety of reasons. First of all, they aren't the virtuoso work of two talented individuals but feature a metaphorical 'cast of thousands.' George Duke, Don Preston, Aynsley Dunbar, and even Jeff Simmons all contribute. As a result, the album has a looser feel than *Hot Rats*, one that feels more like a legitimate jazz session than a simulated jam. This doesn't necessarily mean that *Waka/Jawaka* is better, just different. *Hot Rats* contains a unique combination of composed and improvised music, a balance that appeals both to rock fans who want structure and jazz fans who want free playing. By contrast, *Waka/Jawaka* and *The Grand Wazoo* feature fewer rock structures, with the lengthier tracks being very exploratory. A structure of 'theme-solo-improv' is often followed, which brings the album in line with jazz. Even the shorter vocal-based pieces are unpredictable in structure and melody in a way that may baffle rock listeners unprepared.

Simply put, these albums are Frank's most legitimate jazz-offerings and range from big band, rock riffing, thick brass harmonies, swing, bop, and free improvisation. Unfortunately for the jazz lovers in Frank's audience, these two albums were his last concentrated looks at a genre that he helped create. Thankfully, elements of jazz and improvisation remain in his career but not as focused as on these albums. Fans of these albums who haven't done so should track down copies of *Imaginary Diseases* (2006), *Wazoo* (2007), *One Shot Deal* (2008), and *Little Dots* (2016). *Imaginary Diseases* and *Little Dots* contain selections from the Petite Wazoo band, a 10-member group that played mostly all-original tracks. *One-Shot Deal* contains the Petite Wazoo track 'Trudgin' Across the Tundra.' Those who want to hear the full Grand Wazoo band need to find a copy of *Wazoo* as soon as possible. This 20-member group tackles songs such as 'The Grand Wazoo,' 'Big Swifty,' the infamous 'Approximate,' 'Penis Dimension,' and an early version of 'The Adventures of Greggery Peccary.'

'Big Swifty' (Frank Zappa)

The opening track sets the scene for the rest of the album. Frank's tight guitar riffing and the percussive assault catches the ear, especially when Frank doubles the riff with brass. The call and response is invigorating and helps rock listeners wary of jazz get into the swing of things. The musical content here is a telling example of how well Frank varies up meters.

For example, he rather cleverly switches between a 7/8 and a 3/4 theme in the opening. As 7/8 is just an eighth note more than a typical 3/4, the themes mesh well and the drumming and percussion – as well as the adventurous arranging – create a smooth sound. The tempo continually changes in ways that make the listener glad Frank hired a lot of studio pros: the fact that this album was hammered out in five days is astonishing.

A hint of F# Phygrian plays in the opening with E Dorian in the bass. The outro plays in E Dorian, which shows how clever Frank was in keeping his compositions coherent. After the initial theme – which includes parallels and arpeggios in descant chords creating a modern classical feel – the piece falls into a lengthy free section.

When listening to it, I always feel as if I am floating in space as time stops. Rhythm seems suspended (though there are drums throughout) as horn solos, keyboard lines, guitar parts, bass riffs, and more float in and out of the mix. The sound is unlike anything else in Zappa's catalog and makes it an astonishing listen decades later. The many released live versions of this composition showcase many different instrumental approaches during this section.

'Your Mouth' (Frank Zappa)

The shortest track features singer is Kris Peterson with instrumentation from Zappa, Tony Duran, George Duke, Sal Marquez, Joel Pesin, Mike Atschul, Erroneous, and Aynsley Dunbar. How are the lyrics? Here's the first verse:

> *Your mouth is your religion*
> *You put your faith in a hole like that?*

*You put your trust and your belief
Above your jaw, and no relief
Have I found*

Clearly, Frank is angry. Later verses reveal it is likely to be a lover or, at the very least, a woman:

*An evil woman can make ya cry
If you believe her every time she lies
Well you can be a big fool
If she makes you lose your cool, and so
I've got me some advice you should try*

Though short, this track isn't quite as simple as the average Top 40 hit. First of all, the time signature is 12/8, and the key is in C Dorian, and unlike most pop songs there is no chorus. Instead, Peterson sings the lyrics to the same melody as verse after verse spill out angrily demeaning the lying target of the song. The instrumental backing embellishes the theme with free interjections from the players. This touch ensures that there's always something interesting going on in the song.

'It Just Might Be a One-Shot Deal' (Frank Zappa)

The second vocal tune features Frank on acoustic guitar and 'electric bed springs' alongside Tony Duran, Jeff Simmons, legendary session player 'Sneaky Pete' Kleinow, Sal Marquez, Erroneous, and Aynsley Dunbar. Dunbar plays washboard with Simmons playing Hawaiian guitar. Vocals are shared among Zappa, Duran, Simmons, Marquez, Erroneous, and Janet Ferguson, who was in Zappa's circle for years and who appeared in *200 Motels*. Three main themes appear, broken up with intermezzo sections. The first theme starts the song in E Mixolydian and plays out in swing-time with a 4/4 beat. Duran's slide guitar sounds great as horns pop up to punctuate the chorus in loose harmony.

The piece has a slow and lazy feel with various improvised harmonies from the horn players, who add great embellishments. The first part goes on for about a minute before the second theme comes in with a G-heavy bass line. Once the theme changes, the beat increases in intensity, though the tempo remains consistent. The theme ends at 1:24 when the first intermezzo plays. At this point, the song goes chromatic with a fairly atonal feel that includes electronically-treated vocals that climax at 1:48. The second theme appears again but played as a beautiful slide guitar solo from 'Sneaky Pete.' This interlude is punctuated with fine acoustic work from Frank. Honestly, this whole section could come right from a country or country-rock album – that Zappa diversity once again rearing its beautiful head.

The second intermezzo occurs at 3:18 with a chromatic riff from Frank and free playing by the rest of the band. The last 30 seconds of the song play a new vocal theme played over – and doubled on guitar – over the backing music from the first theme. Frank sings.

'Waka/Jawaka' (Frank Zappa)

This instrumental closer ends things in a rousing manner. Of all the tracks on the album, this feels the closest to *Hot Rats* with its more composed sound. There are several themes, including the opening section, which gets repeated twice before moving on to variations. The second repetition of this theme uses richer instrumentation, including new horn calls.

This theme includes seventh chords and fourths, with the time signature stuck in 4/4 to make the track easier for the players. Throughout this first thematic development, listeners will hear bass counterpoint in A Lydian. After a minute of this theme, Marquez plays a beautiful one-minute trumpet solo, starting in F Major before playing in various modes. A three-minute solo from Don Preston follows as he attempts to tame the mini Moog once again. He tends to stick to F#minor, creating a surprising contrast with Marquez's triumphant solo.

Frank then solos for about two minutes, choosing A Mixolydian as his primary scale before delving into G Mixolydian. These scales were two of Frank's favorites, and this solo is surprising, creative, and memorable. At about 6:31 to 6:44, the second theme pops up in A Lydian mode. This theme contrasts with, but also compliments, the first theme's rhythm before the third theme occurs. This soaring melody creates a feeling of uplift and crescendo and is attractive. After the theme is over, Dunbar solos from about 7:22 to 8:02 before the first theme repeats to create a stronger sense of coherency.

The second theme follows from 9:07 to 9:19, but Zappa transposes it down a major third to create more harmonic depth. Interestingly, Frank cleverly changes the pedal notes around to turn the scale to D Dorian. Zappa then surprises the listener by adding a fourth theme from 9:19 to 9:45. This melody has two phrases that bear harmonic relation to past themes but, melodically, vary them. True music nerds will dig the appearance of C Locrian, a scale rarely used. The second theme then appears transposed up a minor third to create a dramatic shift in the tonal center. After all of these variations, the track plays out from 10:35 to 11:19 with a new theme played in D Major. Frank likely chose a major key because it creates a triumphant sound.

The Grand Wazoo (1972)
Personnel:
See track reviews for detailed personnel listings
Producer: Frank Zappa
Engineer: Kerry McNabb
Recorded Between April 17 and 21
Released: November 27, 1972

The Grand Wazoo was recorded during the same sessions as *Waka/Jawaka*, though it has a slightly different feel. It features a larger array of musicians playing live and overdubbing. This creates one of the largest sounds on any Zappa album, and the personnel listing changes for each track. This is why I'll state who plays on each track during the song reviews. The biggest change is a significant drop in rock-oriented sounds. Though there were a few pop songs on the earlier album and a heavy assortment of recognizable rock riffs, these all but disappear on this record. Instead, there is a heavier emphasis on brass, woodwinds, and freer playing. The arrangements seem loose as the players get more freedom of choice. As a result, there are some strange, atonal, and dissonant moments that pair with coherent and tightly-arranged sections that update big band sounds with a touch of Zappa guitar. This sometimes 'free jazz big band' sound is unique for Zappa and for most rock musicians.

The result is an album that may alienate some fans. Online reviewer George Starostin praised *Waka/Jawaka* on his review site with a 7 out of 10 while bashing *The Grand Wazoo* with a much lower grade. However, jazz review site 'All Jazz' claimed that 'The Grand Wazoo is one of the most playful, scatology-free and accessible big band jazz/rock CDs that Zappa—or anyone else—recorded.' Whatever one's opinion of the album, it is clear that Zappa had achieved something unique, something that he would never pursue again. And fans who enjoy Frank's earlier jazz albums may not like this album. One has to have a high tolerance for free music, including styles out of the pop sphere and instead in the wild world of jazz.

The fact that Zappa didn't follow up much on this style is perhaps not surprising when one considers it didn't even place on the Billboard chart. Though Zappa was always striving to push forward and challenge himself and his audience, he was also raising a family and hoped to support them and himself – and his 'serious' music – with his albums. With his next album, he found a sound and a style that fused his desire for originality and jazz denseness with a rock sound. This general style would serve him well in the '70s as he created some of his most popular work.

Note: When the album was re-released in 1995 on Ryko CD, 'For Calvin' and 'The Grand Wazoo' had swapped positions. More modern listeners are likely used to hearing the grander and stirring 'The Grand Wazoo' start things, but tor the sake of historical accuracy, I will review this album as originally presented.

'For Calvin (And His Next Two Hitch-Hikers)' (Frank Zappa)

The original opening track is strange, which is probably why Frank later changed the song order. Rather than the grand sendoff created with the intricate array of percussion, horns, and guitar on 'Big Swifty,' the listener is welcomed with a low-key 12/8 melody that feels like you just walked into a band warming up. The arrangements are loose and dissonant, created by the players playing freely over the main melody. That said, most of these harmonies feel typical of Frank's love of dissonance. Likely, these were composed with directions to play freely. This track features the highest concentration of lyrics on the album:

> *Where did they go?*
> *When did they come from?*
> *What has become of them now?*
> *How much was the leakage*
> *From the drain in the night*
> *And who are those dudes*
> *In the back seat of Calvin's car?*
> *Where did they go?*
> *When they got off the car?*
> *Did they go get a sandwich*
> *And eat in the dark?*

The composed dissonances, tight vocal harmonies, and strange interjections of the horns combine to create an intense instrumental section starting at about 1:30 that features drama, percussion, and some semi-composed horn punches throughout. This all climaxes at about 5:30 or so, when the main melody comes back. Players on this track (and the title song) include:

Mike Altschul: woodwind, Billy Byers: trombone solo, Joanna Caldwell: woodwind, Earl Dumler: woodwind, Aynsley Dunbar: drums, Tony Duran: guitar, Erroneous: bass, Alan Estes: percussion, Fred Jackson: woodwind, Sal Marquez: vocals, trumpet solo, Malcolm McNab: brass, Janet Neville-Ferguson: vocals, Tony 'Bat Man' Ortega: woodwind, Don Preston: Minimoog, Johnny Rotella: Woodwind, Ken Shroyer: brass, Ernie Tack: brass, Frank Zappa: guitar, Bob Zimmitti: percussion

'The Grand Wazoo' (Frank Zappa)

The appealing guitar part opening this track reveals why it later started the album: this feels like an album opener while 'For Calvin' feels like a mid-album track. The guitar work is paired with excellent drumming and bass that supply a supple jazz feel. After about a minute, the horns start doubling up Frank's solo to create a rich sound. Beneath these horns, richer arrangements provide a harmonic bed that feels very Ellington in harmonic language but with a feel for modern classical. At about 1:38, a second horn theme comes in with a stately pomp mostly missing on the rest of this album. It climaxes several times before the guitar theme comes back at 2:14. This simple, but snappy, theme serves as the musical basis for a significant portion of the track's development.

Several solos, including a Tony Duran bottleneck exploration, shake up the track for a while. The horns take turns coming up with wild noises, while Dunbar produces a percussive drive. This section finishes with a wild Dunbar solo before the first theme recurs with new harmonies. More guitar work is present throughout this section, which gradually develops into the second theme. Again, Zappa places more emphasis on guitar to create a different sonic atmosphere. This rephrasing lasts till 11:45, at which point the theme is once again repeated with new arrangement details. Wild synth sounds pop up near the end of the track.

'Cletus Awreetus-Awrightus' (Frank Zappa)

While previous tracks had varying time signatures, 'Cletus Awreetus-Awrightus' sticks to a stable 4/4. The biggest tweak of this piece is the multitude of themes and key changes that ensure the shortest track on the album still has plenty going on musically.

The first three bars feature a horn-based theme, triumphant in its tones. The strange chord sequence is worth pointing out: A-Bm-C#m-Dm-C#dim5-Bdim5-A. You won't hear chords like that on most pop songs. Frank slams into a deep brass and bass theme after this theme that plays in G Dorian. Parallel octaves are not avoided but the ninth bar changes over to E Mixolydian. The third theme immediately follows, with a similar feel to the first but moving in different directions. Frank cleverly combines bass notes with the chords to create a unique combination of sounds. A sustained Bm chord at about 0:20 seconds into the track transitions to a guitar-heavy section that moves on to the fourth theme, a one-bar phrase that repeats twice.

The themes are repeated in various combinations with different harmonies, though a fifth theme does occur before disappearing for good. A 30-second burst of improvisation keeps the track moving and to the abrupt end. The dizzying array of themes and sounds on this track make it an excellent listen for the serious music listener. Players on this song include:

Mike Altschul: woodwind, 'Chunky': vocals, George Duke: keyboards, vocals, Erroneous: bass, Aynsley Dunbar: drums, Sal Marquez: brass, Ken Shroyer: trombones, Frank Zappa: vocals, guitar, Ernie Watts: C Melody Saxophone solo

'Eat That Question' (Frank Zappa)

This track starts with gorgeous George Duke keyboard arpeggios that show why Frank kept him around for so many years. Duke is a beast and plays excellent, snappy, and never-boring licks for about 30 seconds before he moves to the main riff. He plays this unaccompanied before the guitar and band kick into gear. Rock fans could definitely get behind this riff, as it has a definite blues feel. Duke starts up another keyboard solo at 1:16 after the riff drops, leaving just he and Dunbar and Erroneous. I could listen to George Duke solo for days and never get bored, so this moment is sublime for me.

Duke and Dunbar play off of each other expertly as George begins raining notes on the listener. Its tracks like these that justify the invention of the electric piano: even the most rabid anti-electric piano fan could appreciate Duke's always wonderful playing on the instrument. At 3:18, Zappa takes over and begins a fine solo. Duke stays underneath of Frank, comping, vamping, and adding harmonies. Dunbar remains on fire. What he plays is perhaps not strict jazz drumming, but his endless energy and variations keep the rhythm engaging.

The solo abruptly ends with arrays of synthesizer noises, free drumming, bursts of guitar noise, and a near cessation of all momentum. In the void, Zappa plays the main riff, tweaking it by slowing the rhythm and giving Duke, Erroneous, and Dunbar the chance to add their own embellishments. Just when the track seems done, the main riff recurs with heavier guitar and with denser and more elaborate horn harmonies. Trills of horns create a dramatic feel as the track fades out. Zappa's re-conceptualization of the riff helps keep the track diverse. A full list of players here include:

Mike Altschul: woodwind, George Duke: keyboards, Aynsley Dunbar: drums, Erroneous: bass, Sal Marquez: brass, Joel Peskin: woodwind, Frank Zappa: guitar, percussion, Lee Clement: gong

'Blessed Relief' (Frank Zappa)

The album ends with a soft piece of jazz. At least that's how it feels initially. A light improv starts this waltz-based piece. The improvisation plays in Bb Lydian out before an F Major theme pops in with chords that imply the next segment while staying in key. This clever composition is not unusual in jazz or classical music but only the highest-level pop and rock composers bother with it. The feel of this first theme is soft with a gentle Zappa guitar part probing the horns and driving them. The second theme has a similar feel but shifts into Bb Lydian. Other keys played include A Dorian, G Dorian, F# Dorian, and E Major. The last few keys pop up during the solo segment, which starts at 1:12 and lasts until 6:17. Every four bars, a new scale enters. This complex arrangement creates an array of harmonies. After the solo, Frank repeats the four themes, in order, before more improvisation.

The keyboard arpeggios by Duke are particularly nice and provide a spacey feel that contrasts with the horn and woodwinds. There's something very Earthy about the sounds the players get out of their instruments, suggesting relaxing days in the sun on a beautiful field of grass with nothing better to do than watch the clouds make shapes. Unlike the strum-und-drang of 'Waka/Jawaka,' 'Blessed Relief' provides a sense of relaxation and comfort after a complex and fascinating album. The melodies come closer to the luxuriant haze of a Billy Strayhorn composition than they do standard big band jazz. The players on this track include:

Mike Altschul: woodwind, George Duke: keyboards, Aynsley Dunbar: drums, Tony Duran: rhythm guitar, Erroneous: bass, Sal Marquez: brass, Joel Peskin: woodwind, Frank Zappa: lead guitar

Overnite Sensation (1973)

Personnel:
Frank Zappa: guitar, vocals
Kin Vassy: vocals on 'I'm The Slime', 'Dinah-Moe Humm' and 'Montana'
Ricky Lancelotti: vocals on 'Fifty-Fifty' and 'Zomby Woof'
Sal Marquez: trumpet, vocals on 'Dinah-Moe Humm'
Ian Underwood: clarinet, flute, alto saxophone, tenor saxophone
Bruce Fowler: trombone
Ruth Underwood: percussion, marimba, vibraphone
Jean-Luc Ponty: violin, baritone violin
George Duke: synthesizer, keyboards
Tom Fowler: bass
Ralph Humphrey: drums
Tina Turner and the Ikettes: backing vocals (uncredited)
Producer: Frank Zappa
Engineers: Fred Borkgren, Steve Desper, Terry Dunavan, Barry Keene, Bob Stone
Recorded on March 19 through June 1, 1973
Released: September 7, 1973
Peak Chart Position: Number 32 on the Billboard 200

Frank Zappa's musical career up to and including 1973 had been a whirlwind including groundbreaking production and compositions, innovative instrumental techniques, satirical and sometimes satorical lyrics, and a pattern of album releases paired with and grueling tours. And after seven years of hard work, Zappa was close to exhausted and broke, barely able to pay his band and himself. The Flo and Eddie era had seen some increase in commercial popularity – mostly through heavy concert attendance – but was often silly, complex, and insular. The excellent jazz fusion of the previous two albums was rewarding for Frank and garnered some notice from critics and serious composers, but did not put food on his table.

These issues combined with Frank's continued annoyance with an alleged counterculture movement that had collapsed. Though some 'never say die' hippies existed, many of these so-called revolutionaries fell into drug abuse or fell into line with the world against which they had once rebelled. By the 1980s, many former hippies became yuppies and heavy supporters of Ronald Reagan's policies. These factors pushed Zappa to take an interesting approach to his next album, one that would make his music more mainstream while also maintaining complex approaches and improvisation. It was a move one critic called '...an atrocity committed on a counter-culture now revealed as hypocritical and collusive.'

Frank now focused on compact tracks that featured a maximum of musical ideas in basic rock and pop song structures. Riffs would become the main focus with the smutty lyrics contained in the Flo and Eddie era becoming, generally, more clever and subtle. To achieve this effect, Zappa utilized rock, jazz, pop, blues, and modern classical music. This stylistic jumble provided a fine working environment for Zappa, who then eliminated the harsh dissonances, avant-textures, and lengthy instrumental segments. Zappa becomes the main lead singer for the first time in his career, showing off his newly-deepened voice. However, a multitude of more expressive and expansive singers occur throughout his career to expand upon his limited range.

The result is an album that Robert Christgau gave a C, declaring, 'where's the serious stuff?' with *Rolling Stone* magazine declaring Zappa a spent force creatively. Modern recent reviews, however, have praised the album as a bold reimagining of Zappa's original style, one that simultaneously appealed to more people while pushing the boundaries of the rock format. One reviewer claimed the album's sound was a 'heavy metal hybrid of Louis Jordan and Fats Waller.'

The resulting album went gold three years later and provided Zappa with a multitude of great material to perform for the rest of his career. This album and the next were recorded at the same sessions and were two of his most streamlined, popular, and memorable albums. And key to that is the excellent musicianship of the assembled band. Though the original Mothers were more innovative, this new band is arguably one of Frank's best. Their fluency in multiple genres allowed Frank to combine styles in surprising ways, play his deftly arranged style without strain, and make everything feel funky and catchy.

'Camarillo Brillo' (Frank Zappa)

Any Zappa fan thrilled by the previous two albums was likely to have immediately felt disgusted when hearing this simple pop song. 'Camarillo Brillo' is the perfect example of Zappa's new approach, and he started the album with it to make a point. The music here is based on a fine instrumental arrangement that mixes slide guitars, percussion, horn punctuation, and basic chord progressions. Over the top of this collage of music elements, Frank sings a tale of sex and lust that features somewhat tame sexualized themes:

She stripped away
Her rancid poncho
An' laid out naked by the door
We did it till we were un-concho
An' it was useless any more

The forced rhyme of 'un-concho' reveals the sillier side of Zappa's humor and the vocal melodies range between the rise and fall of the verse and the punchier chorus. The riffs play in the key of E and feature chord progressions such as 'I-V-IV-II-VI.' The chorus is in D to provide harmonic depth. The main joy of the song lies in the arrangement. The percussion of the oft-underrated Ralph Humphrey stops and starts on a dime, and Tom Fowler's bass work remains the definition of dazzling understatement. And the horns provide a nice layer of R&B to give the song a funky feel.

'I'm the Slime' (Frank Zappa)
Though some critics and reviewers would argue that Zappa's satirical style died with the original Mothers, he was still capable of sharp lyrics. His 'rapped' verses about television remain relevant:

You will obey me while I lead you
And eat the garbage that I feed you
Until the day that we don't need you
Don't go for help . . . no one will heed you
Your mind is totally controlled
It has been stuffed into my mold
And you will do as you are told
Until the rights to you are sold

Fans of Zappa's freer side get a taste in the improvised introductory guitar solo over alternating 12/8 and 4/4 meters. The solo moves through different keys, including F# Dorian, E Dorian, and D Dorian. The guitar solo that ends the track uses similar scales but drops many of the notes to create harmonic tension.

After the introduction, a fairly simple bass, keyboard, and drum vamp underpins Zappa's vocals. Before the chorus, interjections of tuned percussion played by Ruth Underwood create diversity in the arrangement. The horns pop up to support the lengthy ending guitar solo. The relative simplicity of the music enhances the message of the song by providing a clearer reading of the lyrics.

'Dirty Love' (Frank Zappa)
'Dirty Love' continues a theme of sexual deviancy common. However, the lyrics are tame and non-descriptive, unlike the smutty, but detailed, lyrics of Flo and Eddie. The only real hint at true smut comes in the references to poodles:

Give me your dirty love
Just like your mama
Make her fuzzy poodle do
Give me your dirty love
The way your mama
Make that nasty poodle chew

The verse chords follow an unusual two-chord vamp, playing I and the VII in D Mixolydian. The simplicity of the chords is enhanced with the arrangement, with violin, keyboard, and percussion flourishes adding countermelodies.

Guitar pops up during the second half of the verse melody to add a little speed. At about 30 seconds into the song, Frank adds a second theme played with C, D, and E7 chords. These thematic changes provide something like a chorus to the song, as it climaxes with more descriptions of 'dirty love' that resolve back into the verse chords and melodies. A brief guitar solo halfway through the song provides a little diversion as the ending 'the poodle bites, the poodle chews it' refrain ends things abruptly.

'Fifty-Fifty' (Frank Zappa)
Fans wanting something a little more complex than 'Dirty Love' likely love 'Fifty-Fifty' but may not appreciate the vocal approach of Ricky Lancelotti. This is one of only a handful of songs that utilized the wild-voiced singer. However, his screaming vocal approach was beyond Zappa's capabilities and suits the tone of the song:

> *Ain't gonna sing you no love song*
> *How my heart is all sore*
> *Will not beg your indulgence*
> *'Cause you heard it before*

Frank is mocking the ridiculous excesses of rock and forces Lancelotti deep into the basement of his range and up towards Robert Plant – or even Geddy Lee – pitches. It is a shame that Lancelotti didn't have more of a chance to sing because his unhinged style could have produced a fun rock album. Musically, the track features great George Duke keyboard parts, a fast pace, multiple themes, and a series of organ, violin, and guitar solos in multiple Mixolydian scales. The band is on fire with Humphrey and Fowler pushing the song. Had Frank wanted to become a straight rocker with this lineup, he wouldn't have had much difficulty.

'Zomby Woof' (Frank Zappa)
Zappa's winning complexity streak continues. The playing, arrangements, and melodic content veer towards prog levels but with increased harmonic sophistication and lyrics dedicated to zombie werewolves rather than flying purple wolfhounds. How complex is the song? Three themes occur in just the first eight seconds. These use fast 16th note runs, abrupt texture and instrumentation changes, and much more. At about eighteen seconds, Zappa starts singing over a distorted Tom Fowler bass riff. This basic theme plays out until about 30 seconds when a fourth theme pops in over 2/4 before the second theme reappears.

The riffs here are among the best on the album as the horns and guitar play a rise-and-fall theme in a subdivided 3/4 signature. Or is that a 3/8? Commentators are split, which underlines the complexity of the song. Frank mostly plays diatonic here – the atonal music of the past is abandoned – though the notes used throughout vary in unpredictable ways. Variations of these themes and riffs recur, including changes into 6/4, 5/4, 5/16, and more.

Lancelotti comes in about a minute as the titular zombie woof. More sung themes occur with the band supporting each with the ease and grace that they brought to every performance.

'Dinah-Moe Humm' (Frank Zappa)

The most sexual track on the album is likely the most controversial. The other sex-based songs were relatively restrained compared to this lengthy track. Just a few samples of the dirty lyrics include:

> *I whipped off her bloomers 'n stiffened my thumb*
> *An' applied rotation on her sugar plum*
> *I poked 'n stroked till my wrist got numb*
> *But I still didn't hear no Dinah-Moe Humm,*
> *Dinah-Moe Humm*

The listener's enjoyment will vary. The backing track is a vamp in 4/4 based on an Em chord with an E pedal note. There are some Zappa-style touches throughout, including a chromatic riff in the sung segments. However, the majority of the musical touches come in the lengthy spoken-word bridge. Here, the band plays around with a simple groove, adding personal touches that provide the track much musical enjoyment. It is here that one hears Tina Turner and the Ikettes on backing vocals; an amusing historical side note mostly buried is that when Ike heard the track, he hated it, insisted on getting paid upfront, and told Frank to remove any reference to the singers from the album credits.

'Montana' (Frank Zappa)

'Montana' alternates fairly complex bits of music with relatively straight sections. The opening segment of fast-paced horn, drum, and bass riffs was so difficult to play that, in the second volume of *You Can't Do That On Stage Anymore*, the band repeatedly makes mistakes and complains about it being too fast, at which point Frank slows the tempo to a funeral dirge. The hardest part occurs when Ruth and Ralph play two very difficult and memorable drum parts to end the introduction. After this George starts playing a fairly simple theme in B Mixolydian, over a VII-I progression. After four bars Duke phases to an A Mixolydian for four bars, two bars of C Mixolydian, and a change to an Em-A-Dm-G chord progression.

This setup recurs after a brief vocal and percussion interlude ('raising my lonely dental floss') before the chorus ('moving to Montana soon') played in B Mixolydian. After the chorus, Frank plays a fine blues-influenced F# Mixolydian solo. During this lengthy interlude, sped-up vocals sing a complex variation of the main themes with the percussion and keyboards backing the melody. Those vocals are the Ikettes, though Napoleon Murphy Brock made the part his own on subsequent tours. The song ends with a repetition of 'moving to

Montana soon' as a pitch-shifted voice shouts 'yippe ki yo ki yay!' over and over again. The lyrics, which focus on making light fun of the rural dreams of many hippies, show a light and absurd touch.

Apostrophe (') (1974)
Personnel:
Frank Zappa: vocals, guitar, bass, bouzouki
Lynn (Linda Sims): vocals, backing vocals
Robert 'Frog' Camarena: vocals, backing vocals
Ruben Ladron de Guevara: vocals, backing vocals
Debbie: vocals, backing vocals
Ray Collins: backing vocals
Sue Glover: backing vocals
Kerry McNabb: backing vocals, engineer, remixing
Sal Marquez: trumpet
Ian Underwood: saxophone
Napoleon Murphy Brock: saxophone, backing vocals
Bruce Fowler: trombone
Don 'Sugarcane' Harris: violin
Jean-Luc Ponty: violin
Ruth Underwood: percussion
George Duke: keyboards, backing vocals
Tony Duran: rhythm guitar
Tom Fowler: bass guitar
Erroneous: bass guitar
Jack Bruce: bass on 'Apostrophe'
Ralph Humphrey: drums
Johnny Guerin: drums on 'Excentrifugal Forz'
Aynsley Dunbar: drums on 'Uncle Remus' and 'Stink-Foot'
Jim Gordon: drums on 'Apostrophe'
Producer: Frank Zappa
Engineer: Barry Keene
Recorded in January 1974
Released: March 22, 1974
Peak Chart Position: Number 10 on the Billboard Top 200

The follow-up to *Overnite Sensation* is a Frank Zappa solo album, whereas the former album was a Mothers album. What are the differences between the two labels at this point in his career? Frank typically brings in more backing musicians on a solo album while a Mothers album features a stable lineup. However, the majority of the material recorded here originated in the same sessions as the previous album.

Whatever the distinction, this fairly short album provides both a more abstract expansion of the style on *Overnite* and a surprising amount of commercial success. At this point, Frank was releasing albums on Warner Brothers, and their release of the longer version of 'Don't Eat the Yellow Snow' was Frank's first Top 100 single success, peaking at 86. The album itself reached the Top 10 in America, making it his most commercially successful album there. To celebrate,

Frank held a parade in honor of Warner Brothers, praising the label's success. This parade is ironic considering Zappa's later troubles with the label. Regardless, this album is one of his most successful and popular albums, which is a nice bit of subversive irony when one examines the music and lyrics.

Frank was making the Billboard Top 100 using an excerpt from a nearly 20-minute suite focused on mocking imperial perceptions of ethnic cultures and religious obsessions, presented as constantly changing and challenging music. The twists and turns on the album may not peak Zappa, but its success probably did more to introduce strange music to the masses than his previous albums. This success is comparable to that of John Waters' *Hairspray*. Though his earlier films like pushed movie boundaries more excessively, Waters maintains that *Hairspray* is his most subversive film. He states that his earlier films were 'preaching to the choir,' but the more mainstream approach of this straighter movie introduced underground concepts to a wider audience.

Sexual humor is almost absent as the lyrics focus on an absurdist form of satire and heartfelt examinations of racism. Whether Zappa cut the sex to appeal to more people or just happened to be more socially-oriented for the album is up to debate. As for the music, soul, pop, rock and roll, jazz, and more mix in a hodgepodge album that doesn't hold together as well as the ones that surround it. However, it remains an engaging listen.

'Don't Eat the Yellow Snow' (Frank Zappa)
Listeners who enjoyed the single version of 'Don't Eat the Yellow Snow' may have been surprised to hear this much shorter version. This situation is interesting because most single versions are edited down. By contrast, Zappa's single version of 'Don't Eat the Yellow Snow' comprised multiple elements from the first four tracks into an interesting distillation of the album. The opening wind sounds on this version create an effect similar to that on The Residents' masterpiece *Eskimo*. The rising and falling bass riff supports the song and moves between 4/8 and 6/8 meters. The simple vocal melody is sung just fine by Frank as a few descending instrumental parts up the tempo without interrupting the groove.

Fans of Zappa's 'serious' music may be dismayed to hear him singing about Eskimos and husky dogs peeing in snow. The novelty approach of the track may be grating, understandably, but the high-quality musicianship on the album should keep most listener's attention. And those who don't like Zappa's smutty humor may find simple absurdities a breath of fresh air.

'Nanook Rubs It' (Frank Zappa)
A descending guitar and bass melody expand on the previous track and the lyrical theme from the first track. Throughout the vamp, Frank describes Nanook's disgust upon seeing his favorite seal being beaten by a fur trapper.

To protect the seal, Nanoonk rubs yellow snow into the trapper's eye to blind him. Nanook is then similarly blinded by the angry fur trapper. Frank was obviously playing with the idea of the ridiculous concept album by creating an absurd situation. The music follows suit, with climaxes and interjections that punctuate the spoken word segments. This approach is one that Frank took often: spoken word segment skits with superlative interrupting segments.

'St. Alfonzo's Pancake Breakfast' (Frank Zappa)

Here, the first place of dazzling musicianship pops up on the album. Ruth Underwood, arguably Frank's finest tuned percussionist, plays a burst of vibe notes based on multiple chords expanded to fifth and ninth chords. As the theme grows – and Ruth pushes herself to the limit – synthesizers join in on harmony before climaxing with a horn fanfare. The rest of the track is a call-and-response affair. Frank sings one bar of lyrics answered by various instrumentals. Common combinations include bass and drums, percussion and guitar, and keyboards and horns.

This approach presents two compositions at once: if you edit out the instrumental interludes, the vocals flow smoothly while the interludes themselves create a complex melody. The lyrics describe the pancake breakfast in the title while throwing in just a touch of sexual humor. Chanting 'hurt me, hurt me' is about as deviant as Frank gets here.

'Father O'Blivion' (Frank Zappa)

This fast-paced tune ends the Eskimo suite with tight unison bass riffing over an E Mixolydian guitar riff with another harmonizing with the main riff. Frank sings of the pancake breakfast as the instruments stop, start, and change nicely without breaking a sweat. Though the instrumental parts aren't complex, the fast tempo makes an impressive ending.

'Cosmik Debris' (Frank Zappa)

This tune is a signature piece for Zappa, showing up on many live albums including tracks from the 1984 band featuring Ike Willis humorously screaming 'HI HO SILVER!' We get blues here, which is a form that becomes increasingly rare for Frank later in his career. The opening guitar riff and solo play in C Dorian, though alternate versions feature the opening riff played on the horn section before the guitar. Having heard this alternate version, the somewhat abrupt beginning on this version makes a bit more sense.

Frank arranges the song in a clever way by keeping the bass line on C. This means he can create multiple chords by contrasting the harmony of basic chords the bass. For example, though the chord progression is simple, the bass creates C7, Eb, G, C, F, and Bbsus2 chords. This change makes a laidback track a bit more complex. The Ikettes pop up as Frank shreds pseudo-new-age guru types to bits. Though the basic vamp throughout the verse doesn't change much, the charming bits of percussion and horns in the chorus provide a welcome change of pace. And the lengthy riff-based bridge, in which Frank demoralizes the fortune teller, creates a nice change.

'Excentrifugal Forz' (Frank Zappa)

This brief side opener provides a surprising amount of instrumental dexterity and arrangement imagination. It starts out in A Mixolydian and is based on a bass riff that provides the main musical feature. The odd synthesizer and keyboard textures create an uneasy feeling as Frank speaks-sings in an odd meter. Fifths are used heavily throughout this track with parallel notes on a bass pedal. A5 chords repeat over a 4/4 meter with addition instrumentation include saxophones, more synthesizers, and what appears to be a distorted violin. The resulting track is queasy – in a good way – and a bit of an oddity.

'Apostrophe' (Frank Zappa, Jim Gordon, Jack Bruce)

This instrumental is a jam with Frank Zappa, Cream's Jack Bruce, and session drummer Jim Gordon. Or is it? Though Bruce is credited on the track, he later stated that his involvement with the track was only the cello part. Bruce was dismissive about the experience:

> *I'm listening to [Zappa's] music, pretty awful, and just don't know what to do with myself, and Frank says to me: 'Listen, I would like you to play a sound, like this... whaaaaaang!!!' So I did what he asked me to do. Whaaaaaang!!! That was all. That was my input to Frank Zappa's most popular record!*

Zappa later stated that the jam was a collaboration because Zappa was friends with Gordon, who was touring with Bruce at the time. Zappa stated that he had difficulty playing with Jack because he was 'too busy' as a bass player, stating that he 'has other things on his mind' than the root functions of bass. This comment is interesting when comparing Zappa's success with Patrick O'Hearn on 'The Ocean is the Ultimate Solution,' a track with a much busier bass track. Likely, that track was composed, or semi-composed, or O'Hearn simply provided Frank with a better grounding for his soloing.

So, is Bruce on the track? This writer, who is quite familiar with Bruce's bass playing and music – and a huge fan of both – hears 'Wee Jack's' giant fuzz tone all over the track. And those parts are trademark Bruce style. My assumption is that Jack either forgot about the jam or didn't enjoy it. One has to wonder why when hearing how well it comes across. Note: Tony Duran also plays rhythm guitar.

'Uncle Remus' (Frank Zappa, George Duke)

This soulful track feels somewhat out of place on a frantic album. However, its gorgeous music (written by Duke) is matched with a superlative Zappa lyric, one of his most serious, as he explores the state of racism in the country despite the Civil Right Movement:

> We look pretty sharp in these clothes (yes, we do)
> Unless we get sprayed with a hose
> It ain't bad in the day if they squirt it your way
> 'Cept in the winter, when it's froze
> An' it's hard if it hits on yer nose
> Just keep yer nose to the grindstone, they say
> Will that redeem us, Uncle Remus ...
> I can't wait till my Fro is full-grown
> I'll just throw 'way my Doo-Rag at home
> I'll take a drive to BEVERLY HILLS
> Just before dawn
> An' knock the little jockeys off the rich people's lawn

The music here is not quite as obviously complex as Zappa's but filled with great subtle touches. Duke was, in his own right, a fine composer and plays beautiful piano and variations throughout.

'Stink-Foot' (Frank Zappa)

Like 'Montana' before it, 'Stink-Foot' ends the album on a rather strange note. Most of the track is recited, rather than sang, and may feel rather simple. The basic music underlying Frank throughout most of the track is as 12/8 vamp on a C Mixolydian scale. A looseness is present throughout the track, with interjections coming at odd times and providing dramatic accentuation to the lyrics:

> This has to be the disease for you
> Now scientists call this disease Bromidrosis
> But us regular folks
> Who might wear tennis shoes
> Or an occasional python boot
> Know this exquisite little inconvenience
> By the name of: STINK FOOT

Another amusing lyrical moment pops up later towards the end of the song:

> Well then Fido got up off the floor an' he rolled over
> An' he looked me straight in the eye
> An' you know what he said?
> Once upon a time
> Somebody say to me
> (This is a dog talkin' now)
> What is your Conceptual Continuity?

The line 'this is the dog talkin' now' is particularly memorable to many listeners. The track ends with a lengthy recitation of the 'the poodle bites, the poodle chews it' segment from 'Overnite Sensation.' Musically, the track has a bluesy feel that focuses on keyboards, bass, and drums.

Roxy & Elsewhere (1974)

Personnel:
Frank Zappa: lead guitar and vocals
Jeff Simmons: rhythm guitar and vocals
Napoleon Murphy Brock: flute, tenor saxophone, and vocals
George Duke: keyboards, synthesizer, and vocals
Don Preston: synthesizer
Bruce Fowler: trombone, dancer
Walt Fowler: trumpet and bass trumpet
Tom Fowler: bass guitar
Ralph Humphrey: drums
Chester Thompson: drums
Ruth Underwood: percussion
Producer: Frank Zappa
Engineer: Kerry McNabb
Recorded on December 8, 9 & 10 1973 and May 8 & 11, 1974
Released: September 10, 1974
Peak Chart Position: No. 27 on the Billboard Top 200

The success of his previous two albums boosted interest in Zappa's music, though critics were wary of what some – but not all – considered a compromise. However, interest in Frank's music encouraged him to hire a camera crew to film several of his concerts at the Roxy in Hollywood. This film was supposed to highlight his band manner and would be shown in theaters and television. Unfortunately, a mistake was made when recording the sound, and it was impossible to sync. The problem wasn't a single issue with the film speed but multiple mistiming instances. With the technology available at the time, correcting the errors would have been impossible. This film, as a result, sat in the vault for decades and was only released in 2015, when studio technology finally allowed the proper corrections.

Never one to let good material go to waste, Frank listened several nights of tapes and chose the best performances for a live album. He added overdubs including thicker horn arrangements, more keyboards, and sped-up vocals. This approach was not the first, nor the last time Frank would mix the stage and studio. Additional tracks (the 'Elsewhere' of the title) were added to bring the album to just under 69 minutes. These two tracks came from a show at Edinboro Stage College, in Edinboro, Pennsylvania on May 8, 1974. Additional material for 'Son of Orange County' was recorded in the Auditorium Theatre in Chicago, Illinois. The non-Roxy material contains no overdubs.

Almost all of the material here is new and is among Zappa's most complexly composed, arranged, and performed rock music. As always, he mixes genres like rock, funk, jazz, modern classical, pop, and more. However, he ups the complexity of the song structures from the last two albums and uses rougher and more free-flowing structures. And while there are plenty of sung portions, they are balanced by the tightest and most difficult ensemble playing of Zappa's career. But this doesn't feel like empty showboating because the composition techniques are sharp, the playing exciting, and the result not mind-numbing but mind-boggling. It is here that the Mothers Mark 3 make their most impressive mark.

Critics at the time were – as always with Zappa – somewhat ambivalent. Alan Niester of 'Rolling Stone' said 'When Zappa tries (which is rare) he is one fine guitarist, and the rest of the Mothers could doubtless run rings around anyone else in the jazz-rock field if they ever considered it worth their while. Basically, though, you either love Zappa and the Mothers, or you loathe them, and *Roxy & Elsewhere* is still an album for fans only.' Similarly, Robert Christgau said 'You can actually hear Zappa thinking on 'More Trouble Every Day,' and 'Son of Orange County' is an uncommonly understated Nixon tribute. The rest is the usual eccentric clichés, replete with meters and voicings and key changes that are as hard to play as they are easy to forget.' By contrast, modern reviews, particularly from fans, are glowing. On Allmusic, François Couture ends his review by saying 'Compared to the man's previous live recordings (*Fillmore East: June 1971, Just Another Band from L.A.*), this one sounds fantastic, finally providing an accurate image of the musicians' virtuosity. For fans of Zappa's intricate material like 'RDNZL,' 'The Black Page,' or 'Inca Roads,' this album is a must-have.'

Fans of this album should also find the *Roxy By Proxy* release and *The Roxy Performances*, the latter of which contains all the recorded material at the shows, including soundchecks, with no overdubs. Also of interest is the second volume of *You Can't Do That On Stage Anymore*, which contains a full and unedited concert by the same band in Helsinki, Finland.

'Penguin in Bondage' (Frank Zappa)

Frank's opening narration on 'Penguin in Bondage' sets a strange mood. As one of the few sexual tracks on the album, Frank tries to explain what the song is about without saying it revolves around S&M with nuns (the penguins in bondage). Fans weary of Frank's sexual escapades may roll their eyes, but fans of his outward-looking music will appreciate the ways that Zappa twists song conventions. The opening features a barrage of synthesizers, changing tempos and meters, and arrangement details that feel loose but which coalesce.

This version is an edit of two performances, with the guitar solo from one being placed onto the rest of another performance. Frank's by now seamless editing skills makes it nearly impossible to tell when one track begins and another changes. The stop-and-start structure robs the song of 'groove' factor, but the percussion barrages keep the music flowing. And when Zappa bursts into a lengthy blues solo – in D Dorian – fans can relax and listen to his flurry of notes. Frank chooses an interesting tone to create an underwater feel for a solo that creates a consistent mood consistent.

'Pygmy Twylyte' (Frank Zappa)

This track – the shortest on the album – bursts with energy, changes in melody and tempo, wonderful singing from Napoleon Murphy Brock, and the closest we'll get to pop. The horns – many overdubbed – are effective in creating countermelodies that serve as a harmonic bed for Brock's frantic singing. It's this type of song that inspired performers interested in expanding the boundaries of the form with fast-paced, complex, but hummable pop music. England's infamous eccentrics, Cardiacs, likely wouldn't exist without the influence of such tracks. The endless energy, the fine instrumentation, the changes in meter and harmony, and more all coalesce into an unforgettable two minutes.

'Dummy Up' (Brock, Simmons, and Zappa)

This skit track consists of a vamp over which Frank and Napoleon debate the virtues of high school diplomas and college education. This track is an edited version of a lengthy goof that included Jeff Simmons (of all people) on rhythm guitar. He and Don Preston made guest appearances at the Roxy shows and appear sporadically. Frank is trying to sell Napoleon a college education to 'smoke' as a drug. Frank's anti-intellectualism comes out here as he says you get 'nothing with a college education,' a position that many would disagree with heavily. Others may get a laugh out of this track. Brock, for my taste, is wittier than Flo and Eddie, though not quite as outrageous.

'Village of the Sun' (Frank Zappa)

Side two of the original album starts with one of the finest tracks on the album. Ruth Underwood has stated that this is one of her favorite of Frank's songs for its musical structure and its lyrical focus on nostalgia, as Frank describes the song as a remembrance of his life in Palmdale, California.

The track begins with an instrumental prelude with multiple scales variations on E Mixolydian. For example, E Phrygian, A Lydian, and F Lydian – among others – all pop up throughout the early bars. Meters mix between 9/8, 4/4, 6/8, and 5/4. This introduction leads well into the main track, which includes a funky groove over which George Duke sings. George mixes up the chords, including switching a G chord to an Ab chord as he sings lyrics that, while simple, create a nostalgic and even romantic atmosphere:

> *Goin' back home*
> *To the Village of the Sun*
> *Out in back of Palmdale*
> *Where the turkey farmers run, I done*
> *Made up my mind*
> *And I know I'm gonna go to Sun*
> *Village, good God I hope the*
> *Wind don't blow*

Every player does well here, with interjections of tuned percussion, wonderful drum grooves between Chester and Ralph, and Tom Fowler supplying his supple and subtle bass.

'Echidna's Arf (Of You)' (Frank Zappa)

As George intones 'Yeah yeah yeah yeah, villlaaage' the horns start playing a difficult melody of 16th notes that rise, fall, and jump. The band supports this melody with rhythmic intensity and harmonic depth but take things to strange places with polyrhythms. Frank was no stranger to – and quite proud of his use of – polyrhythms in his music. Here, you get a 4/4 melody played over 11/16 segments in a way that creates dramatic variations and conflicts. Zappa often did this in tracks such as 'King Kong,' in which 3/8 melodies play out on 4/4 music and in 'Cruising for Burgers' in which 6/8 plays out over 24/32. In this fast-paced instrumental, Frank mixes Lydian and major scales, including B minor and B Dorian while playing 3/4, 12/8, 4/4, 6/8, 2/3, 12/8, 3/2, and 2/2 at various times. All these twists and turns are intense and transition seamlessly to an even more complex piece.

'Don't You Ever Wash That Thing?' (Frank Zappa)

A quick segue from the previous tracks starts out with a barrage of fast-paced drumming from Chester and Ralph. Horns pop in and out of the arrangement, playing a melody that contrasts with the drumming. These bursts of melody are played in various meters, including 4/16, 5/16, and 9/16. Between each meter break, a segment of 5/8 percussion upsets the melodic and rhythmic movement.

Fans of Zappa's simpler tunes may have been unprepared for this melodic onslaught. The band plays in difficult counterpoint, sometimes with as many as three melodies going at the same time. Typically, you hear the bass playing one line with the drums while the horns and tuned percussion play related, but different, themes. Of particular interest is how Frank gets Tom Fowler to play diatonically on the bass – providing harmonic and melodic stability – while allowing the band to play chromatically. The resulting sound is one equally harmonious and discordant. Like with 'Echidna,' describing the endless changes here would require a music degree. As always with Zappa, there are tempo changes, abrupt shifts into different melodic movements, and humor, as Frank teases Ruth about 'doing something fantastic.' The constantly rising feel, the panicked tempo, and dramatic interludes bring the second side of the album to a stunning close.

'Cheepnis' (Frank Zappa)

After a lengthy introduction where Frank discusses his love of b-movies, we reach what may be the finest moment on the album. 'Cheepnis' is a musical and lyrical tour-de-force that combines the instrumental diversity and flexibility of the instrumental sections with fast-paced – and memorable – melodies and some of Napoleon Murphy Brock's best singing.

Lyrically, you get great stanzas like the following, each of which celebrates the ridiculous nature of b-movies:

> *Little Miss Muffett on a squat by me, yeah*
> *Took a turn around, I said: Can y'all see now?*
> *The little strings on the Giant Spider?*
> *The Zipper From The Black Lagoon?*
> *(HA HA HA!)*
> *The vents by the tanks where the bubbles go up?*
> *(And the flaps on the side of the moon)*
> *The jelly & paint on the 40-watt bulb*
> *They use when the slime droozle off*
> *The rumples & the wrinkles in the cardboard rock, yeah*
> *And the canvas of the cave is too soft*

These lyrics come at a nearly impossible tempo, but Brock tosses the lyrics off as easily as singing the alphabet. He not only hits the notes and sings them well but adds a little interpretation to the lines. Live videos show the explosive singer getting into the song by dancing, mugging, and performing just as tightly as the rest of the band. And the percussion section gets a particular workout. Chester holds down the main rhythm while Ralph goes from his drum set to the timpani, the tuned percussion, and plays off Chester's unnervingly-precise rhythm with ease and aplomb. Ruth stands shoulder-to-shoulder with Ralph and Chester to produce a beautifully-arranged percussion onslaught.

In the Roxy film, the full song is preceded by a percussion-only arrangement, and listeners can hear how well the percussion emphasizes the song. And the other instrumentalists create a constantly changing and melodically-challenging piece that holds together through sheer force of will. Only Frank Zappa could write music like this, and only this band could perform it so easily.

'Son of Orange County' (Frank Zappa)

This dramatically rearranged version of the original Mothers classic goes at a slower tempo that focuses heavily on Zappa's guitar. Frank expands the chords to include seventh, fifth, and eleventh chords. This harmonic expansion provides increased dramatic range in this thick and rich song. The slower pace translates well to a closing rendition of 'Oh No.' This sedate feeling has more in common with R&B than it does rock and creates a change of pace after two sides of high-speed energy.

'More Trouble Every Day' (Frank Zappa)

Another reworked classic, 'More Trouble Every Day' uses new music with slightly updated lyrics to create a whole new track. The music is more complex, spacey, and has a slightly funky-blues feel through the verses and chorus. Every live version of this song released after this album follows this arrangement and not that of the 1966 original. Which version is better? That all depends on taste. Those who love the simpler '60s blues-rock feel of the first may be disappointed in its disappearance here. Those who want a funkier and jazzier sound may dig the change.

'Be-Bop Tango (Of the Old Jazzmen's Church)' (Frank Zappa)

This 16-minute track is one of two tangos released by Frank, including 'Sheik Yerbouti Tango.' The composed elements of this track are complex, including whole-tone scales, mixed 4/4 and 2/4 meters, dissonant and difficult harmonies, and instrumentals so knotty that Eric Dolphy would have approved.

Frank took a typical be-bop melody – sung by Duke in little bursts – and twisted it into an avant shape. Anyone waiting for a melody will be disappointed. However, after a mad Bruce Fowler trombone solo, the rest of the track begins: a dance contest. Tom Fowler plays a very simple bass line over a basic drum beat while Duke's burst of keyboard and singing serves as the background for audience dancing. Unfortunately, this lack of visuals makes this part drag. Anyone who has seen the Roxy movie knows that the dance sequence is funny to watch but listening to it for over 10 minutes gets wearying, even when the band bursts into a mad free improvisation which causes Frank to shout 'Now you're probably thinking to yourself, 'I could do that!' And of course, you're right!'

One Size Fits All (1975)

Personnel:
Frank Zappa: guitar, lead and backing vocals
George Duke: keyboards, lead and backing vocals, synthesizer
Napoleon Murphy Brock: flute, lead and backing vocals, tenor saxophone
Ruth Underwood: marimba, vibraphone, percussion
Chester Thompson: drums, sound effects, voices
Fowler: bass guitar
James 'Bird Legs' Youman: bass guitar
Johnny 'Guitar' Watson: vocals
Captain Beefheart (credited as 'Bloodshot Rollin' Red'): harmonica
Producer: Frank Zappa
Engineer: Kerry McNabb
Recorded Between August 27, 1974 and April 1975
Released: June 25, 1975
Peak Chart Performance: Number 26 on the Billboard Top 200

After the previous album heralded a move out of song-oriented styles, this studio album proved that Frank had pushed the limits of his interest in pop as far as they could go. Touring with this band of ace musicians – and writing difficult music that they could easily play – inspired Zappa to create a richer approach in the studio. Gone are the relatively straight forward pop structures of *Overnite Sensation*, replaced by through-composed works. Sex and even humor are often ejected in favor of more obscure – and even emotional – subjects. And the abstract – but sometimes disjointed – *Apostrophe (')* style of talking-over-vamps was replaced by compact jazz-rock.

Frank's approach on this album sometimes veers towards complex but thoughtful, funk-prog. Zappa adds his own touch to the genre by skillfully mixing in a funkier, bluesier, and more complex arrangement style. Those thrilled by the music but baffled by the lyrics of albums like *Close to the Edge* likely had much to chew on here.

The stately nature of the melodies, the tight-knit arrangements and playing, and the expansive songwriting concepts were not to be explored again. Though Zappa teased a second album – recorded at the same time – the band broke up after a tour as the members moved on in their professional career. This left Zappa without a band, though he was able to bring together some musicians for a tour.

As always, criticism was mixed. Robert Christgau was harsh, stating that Zappa's '...satire has neither improved nor deteriorated' while claiming that his fans had '...gotten bored with his repertoire of stylistic barbarities. Us smart people just got bored faster.' Such implied fan contempt is inaccurate: the album peaked at 26 on the Billboard Top 200 and fan polls regularly rate this record as one of his finest creations.

'Inca Roads' (Frank Zappa)

Fans who saw the Roxy movie may have enjoyed a laid back and sedate blues romp by this name featuring George Duke on vocals and piano. However, the studio version may have taken them a bit by surprise. Though this track is – technically – taken from two live recordings, subtle touch-ups and overdubs create a bizarre master. It is one of several 'through-composed' pieces. For those not familiar with the term, through-composed songs aren't based on repeated sections of music but different music for each section. One example of this is 'Stairway to Heaven' by Led Zeppelin. The song flows through multiple movements and expands on them. 'Inca Roads' does the same.

The first sounds are a tight drum, bass, and xylophone melody interrupted by high-flying George Duke synthesizer. Duke sings the gorgeous melody – with lyrics focusing on UFOs – as the arrangement shifts and churns behind him. After about a minute of this, a very Zappa-like interruption occurs – fast percussion lines, multiple voices chanting strange lyrics, and a fast shift back to the main melody. This interruption bothered George Duke, who said: 'This is such a beautiful melody, do you have to mess it up?' Zappa simply replied 'Yeah, but it needs some messing up.'

The whole of the song features gorgeous melodies interrupted by runs of percussion and saxophone. The lengthy guitar solo towards the middle of the track provides Zappa with a little something to do – guitar is not very prominent on the track otherwise – as the band intones wordlessly over the top. This solo was edited in from another performance. After the solo is over, an abrupt shift into percussion noises and a new melody appears, this time featuring sped up Napoleon Murphy Brock vocals. The song comes to an end with thumping percussion and the phrase 'On Ruth! On Ruth! Haha, that's Ruth!' Time signatures include 8/16, 15/16, and even a few moments of 5/16 and 4/4. The many abrupt interruptions in the main melody make the track seem like a mess, but everything coalesces.

'Can't Afford No Shoes' (Frank Zappa)

'Can't Afford No Shoes' is one of Zappa's finer pure rock songs. The opening riff is a basic A-B-D riff played in a B Mixolydian scale before the verse shifts to E Mixolydian. The track mostly sticks to E throughout and features contrasting verse and chorus melodies that flow smoothly together. The chorus features 15 different chords, five different keys, and a variety of note combinations. Such small touches show what separates Frank from many other rock composers: even when his music seems simple, experimental harmonic and melodic approaches appear.

Frank throws a monkey wrench into the track by including multiple voices commenting on the lyrics and singing in parallel octaves. The result is chaotic but appealing. The parallel octaves – though frowned upon by most composers – don't add extra harmonic depth but create a conflict between Zappa's deep vocals and the higher ones. Note: this track does not feature Tom Fowler on bass, as he broke his hand before recording it.

'Sofa No. 1' (Frank Zappa)
An instrumental version of a track first performed as early as 1971 with the Flo and Eddie era, this gorgeous melody is one of Frank's finest. Like 'Inca Roads,' it has many through-composed elements that flow smoothly and appealingly. Frank put a lot of effort into its harmonies: multiple counterpoint melodies, including independently-moving harmonic lines, enhance the melody. Fans of this track will also likely appreciate the reprise, with vocals, featured at the end of the album.

'Po-Jama People' (Frank Zappa)
'Po-Jama People' is a blues track that starts out with a sharp Zappa guitar solo with some supporting piano chords by Duke. The slow solo feels like you're sitting in a blues lounge and a particularly soulful ballad. As with all things Zappa, this mode isn't touched on very long. At about 0:38, the song shifts to a mostly piano-led attack that features some 'speak-singing' from Zappa. The band supports Duke's piano with lithe and skilled playing, pushing the song and giving it some nice lift. Zappa's guitar drones in the background, threatening feedback, but he has the sucker under control.

This song features a bit of a through-composed feel, though there are moments where the melody repeats itself. However, the basic tune expands in various ways, including sustained notes, changing harmonic beds, and sudden bursts of guitar. Though the band isn't exploring the absolute limits of their playing, they react sharply to the song's twists and turns. Frank's sustained lines on the rising 'hoy hoy hoy!' refrain, provide a hook before a lengthy guitar solo. After the solo, Frank continues to lead the way, playing the sung melodies.

The melody here is different than the opening theme but features similar harmonic settings. The only recurring musical element from the intro is the 'po-jama people' refrain including the 'hoy! hoy! hoy!' guitar melody. The song comes to a close and leaves the listener feeling breathless at the focused blues and jazz energy.

'Florentine Pogen' (Frank Zappa)
'Florentine Pogen' is led by Napoleon Murphy Brock, who deftly navigates the song's odd structure to provide a bit of an anchor for the audience. The opening guitar riff plays in E Minor during the first half before an interruption by the horns playing variations. A shift to C# Lydian occurs in the second half of the theme that provides a feeling of uplift. The melody ascends rather than descends.

Brock sings over a mostly drum-based arrangement before a brief burst of 16th notes leads to the second melody – during this section, only a chromatically-descending bass guitar supports Brock. Interjections with the horn and guitar appear on either side to create the 'stop and start' feeling of the album. The verses use a similar musical backing but with different chords to harmonize the melody. As the song progresses, Brock begins a call-and-response battle with the other vocalists over the word 'pogen,' with him taking 'po' and the rest of the band taking 'gen.' A bridge appears that feels straighter before Brock chants wordlessly until the 'Chester's Gorilla' segment occurs.

Slowed-down vocals create an uncomfortable atmosphere and, during concerts, a man in a gorilla suit came out to bother Chester Thompson, only to be chased away by Brock with a bug sprayer. The track comes to a close on the first verse, set in a slightly different harmonic environment, to provide a comforting return home.

'Evelyn, A Modified Dog' (Frank Zappa)
This brief, but melodic, interlude features a melody that follows the words over a strict eight-note rhythm. Most of the track is in 4/4 with the instruments following the piano and words. The result has a nice effect, though this track cannot be considered a major piece.

'San Ber'dino' (Frank Zappa)
The opening of 'San Ber'dino' feels nearly country and western (!) before the main theme pops up. An instrumental melody comes in mirroring the vocal but with larger and more surprising intervals. After four seconds, the main theme pops up only to be interrupted by two instrumental passages. The main theme reprises with a slight variation before another instrumental block. After a four-second reprise of the main theme, another instrumental occurs before jumping back into the main theme. At the risk of boring the reader, let's skip breaking down every individual theme and melody on this complex track.

Listeners can anticipate country, blues, some R&B, percussion interjections, voices harmonizing, and Frank's hero, Johnny 'Guitar' Watson coming up with some vocal interjections in the outro. The lyrics here are surprisingly romantic:

> *She's in love with a boy*
> *From the rodeo*
> *Who pulls the rope on the chute*
> *When they let those suckers go*
> *(Yeah-hey! Suckers!)*
> *He got slobberin' drunk at the Palomino*
> *They give him thirty days in San Ber'dino*
> *Well there's forty-four men*
> *Stashed away in Tank 'C'*
> *An' there's only one shower*
> *But it don't apply to Bobby*

'Andy' (Frank Zappa)
The penultimate track on the album is one of Zappa's most complex and personal songs of all time. Said to be inspired by his love – or lust – for a

groupie named Andy (which he denied), the lyrics are some of his most personal and revealing:

> *Is there anything good inside of you?*
> *If there is, I really wanna know*
> *Is there anything*
> *Good inside of you?*
> *If there is I really wanna know*

The lyrics feel more like chants or taunts, but the music repeatedly changes, with the vocals following the arrangement. The introduction is a soaring theme focused on a rising and falling guitar riff. Keyboards accentuate it. The basic 4/4 of the theme gives it a normal feel that eases the listener into the strangeness to follow. Thematically, the chords move around an A Lydian with a I-II progression.

The second theme flows in varying meters. Bass and drums lead the way as the singer asks Andy if there is 'anything good inside of you.' At various points, the track stops dead in its track with a sustained synthesizer. These unpredictable breaks give the section a strange feel that breaks up into a third theme. The meter is now a stable 6/8 with the melody played in E in a bluesy idiom. The first theme returns with the basic lyrics imploring Andy to give just one sign of goodness. The fourth theme occurs here as a variation upon the first. The basic rhythm plays with the instruments harmonizing as the song asks 'do you know what I'm telling you, is it really something that you can understand?'

Funk pops over over a C#m6 and F# progression with a C# Dorian harmonic basis. This section ends with a flurry of 16th notes over a D pedal note played in 5/16. These themes combine in multiple ways and in various harmonic guises with the track ending on a new outro guitar riff that feels urgent and exciting. The guitar solo drives the song to the finish like a sprinter going over the finish line.

' **Sofa No. 2**' (Frank Zappa)

Featuring the same arrangement as 'Sofa No. 1' – if not the same backing track – the sung version features slight harmonic variations. Multiple sections have three-party polyphonic harmony in the vocals. The lyrics themselves are quite silly – if very poorly translated into German in parts – and narrated by God sitting on a large sofa smoking a big cigar. How very Zappa.

Bongo Fury (1975)

Personnel:
Frank Zappa: lead guitar, lead and backing vocals
Captain Beefheart: harp, lead and backing vocals, shopping bags (also soprano sax)
George Duke: keyboards, lead and backing vocals
Napoleon Murphy Brock: sax, lead and backing vocals
Bruce Fowler: trombone, fantastic dancing
Tom Fowler: bass, also dancing
Denny Walley: slide guitar, backing vocals
Terry Bozzio: drums, moisture
Chester Thompson: drums (on '200 Years Old' and 'Cucamonga')
Robert 'Frog' Camarena: backing vocals on 'Debra Kadabra' (uncredited)
Producer: Frank Zappa
Recorded on May 20 and 21, 1975 (mostly live) and January 1975 (studio)
Released: October 2, 1975
Peak Chart Position: Number 66 on the Billboard Top 200

After Zappa produced Captain Beefheart's album *Trout Mask Replica*, the relationship between these two high school friends suffered. The Captain accused Zappa of poorly producing the album and of influencing his creativity negatively. He claimed that Zappa wanted to 'make me into a horrible freak' and believed that Zappa's behavior encouraged 'kids out there on the streets' to start taking dope to appreciate his music, claiming that it was '...disgusting and totally degrading that Zappa should do this to me.'

Such harsh words weren't lost on Zappa – who, ironically, was against drug use – and he probably watched with bemusement as Beefheart attempted a more commercial sound after the *Lick My Decals Off, Baby* album. *The Spotlight Kid* and *Clear Spot* slowed down and streamlined the Captain's sound but remained true to his essence by focusing on dark and mysterious blues. By contrast, *Unconditionally Guaranteed* and *Bluejeans and Moonbeams* were critical and commercial disappointments, with Beefheart fans who loved his strangeness very likely disgusted at such simple pop songs like 'Love On My Mind,' and the radio continued to ignore the Captain, having pegged him as a 'freak' years ago.

As a result, Beefheart had no label and no band by 1974 and was in a difficult position. Seeing Zappa's success over the years, he approached his childhood friend and asked for a job. Frank auditioned Beefheart in Halloween of 74:

> He flunked. See, he had a problem with rhythm, and we were very rhythm oriented. Things have to happen on the beat. I had him come up on the bandstand at our rehearsal hall and try to sing 'Willie the Pimp,' and he couldn't get through it. I figured if he couldn't get through that, I didn't stand much of a chance in teaching him the other stuff.

However, Beefheart practiced and improved enough to get in the band, though Zappa lamented that he still had difficulty remembering the words. By this point, the band streamlined to George Duke, Napoleon Murphy Brock, Bruce and Tom Fowler, Denny Walley, and Terry Bozzio, a teenage drumming phenomenon. This band was one of, if not the last, touring Mothers lineups. After the short tour with the Captain, the band – except for Bozzio – would disappear.

The agreement with the Captain included the tour and an album made on Zappa's 'Discreet' label. The tour, though billed as a collaboration between the two, was almost entirely Zappa's music. In fact, Beefheart was rarely used. He occasionally sang songs that were written for him, played a little sax, but mostly sat on the stage drawing. To suit the Captain's range, Zappa utilized bluesy songs, which he felt was an excellent medium for Beefheart. The usable recorded live material was limited, due to recording costs, and the released album has obvious mistakes and imperfections and Beefheart's 'Discreet' album, *Bat Chain Puller*, ended up being derailed by banal royalty issues. These included Cohen, Zappa's manager at the time, paying for the production of the album with Zappa's royalty checks.

Other legal and financial issues delayed the album released until 2012, though Beefheart later released a re-recorded version *Shiny Beast (Bat Chain Puller)*, one of his finest. It utilizes the Captain's strange music ideas in more streamlined and melodic formats without compromising their core oddity. Some parts even veer towards Zappa-like complexity at times. But on *Bongo Fury*, reviewers at the time weren't too impressed. Gordon Fletcher of *Rolling Stone* stated that 'Beefheart's meandering musings usually have all the continuity of a random sample' and that 'the music isn't much better, segueing in and out of conflicting moods with all the subtlety of a brick wall'. He ended by hinting thatthe only reason he didn't name it the worst album of the year was because of Lou Reed's *Metal Machine Music*. Christgau was surprisingly positive, claiming that 'the jazzy music has a soulful integrity' and gave the album a B.

Modern reviews praise the album as a unique entry in Zappa's library due to its bluesy approach. Unlike Christgau, though, who praised the album due to Beefheart, online reviewer George Starostin claimed that the album was his introduction to the singer and that his ragged vocals almost turned him off Beefheart. On Allmusic, a 3.5-star review stated that 'Most Zappa enthusiasts either love or hate *Bongo Fury*' but that '...those consumers whose passions tend toward both Zappa and Captain Beefheart consider this disc as a mutual zenith. Either way, there is a little something for every element.'

Bongo Fury creates a world and sound unique to itself and maintains that atmosphere, in spite of the mixed medium of live and studio tracks. The sometimes dark feel of the album would later be the focus of Zappa's next project, a true solo album that left him without a band for the first time in his career.

'Debra Kadabra' (Frank Zappa)

The first track is a rampaging blues-influenced rocker that features Beefheart at his finest and which may be one of Zappa's most underrated songs. It features a structure that moves very through multiple motifs and melodies. This through-composed track retains a rock-like feel and feels like something Beefheart could have performed on one of his albums. Zappa's Beefheart-style emulation is so impressive that I thought, for years, that it was a particularly focused song by the Captain (who showed with later albums that he could write on a similar level when inspired).

The lyrics, particularly, feel like the poetic ramblings of Vliet, though are credited to Zappa. Frank wanted Beefheart to, eventually, improvise similar lyrics on this tour though Don never reached that level of comfort:

> *Oh Debra Algebra Ebneezra Kadabra!*
> *Witch Goddess, Witch Goddess of Lankershim Boulevard!*
> *Cover my entire body with Avon Cologna*
> *And drive me to some relative's house in East L.A. (Wooden dog!)*
> *Just till my skin clears up!*

Beefheart's approach here is pretty unhinged and ragged but contributes to the appeal of the song. Zappa math-rocks his way through this one, with 4/4, 5/8, 12/8, 14/8, 11/8, and 12/6 motifs appearing. And while the melodic elements include a bluesy feel, including Am7 chords, A Dorian scales, and F# progressions, the madness creates something entirely different.

'Carolina Hard-Core Ecstasy' (Frank Zappa)

After the madness of the opening track, this second Zappa-sung track is a relief. Featuring a very blues-like atmosphere and fine saxophone embellishments, this track is nearly romantic in the Zappa idiom. The 4/4 meter stays consistent, and the basic C-Em-Am7-D chord progression varies only slightly throughout by tweaking the bass root notes. When it came to writing for bass, Frank was one of the cleverest composers in rock. He would alter the underlying bass guitar notes to combine with a basic chord progression in surprising ways. This approach let him subtly change the music while maintaining a simpler and basic appeal.

A very fine blues guitar solo ends this piece, and though the instrumental fireworks of the last few albums are gone, Zappa compensates with excellent guitar solos that begin to approach the level of excellence he would show in the late '70s.

'Sam with the Showing Scalp Flat Top' (Don Van Vliet)

This track is a Beefheart poem with some rather tense and brooding backing music. The poem is strange and includes the phrase 'I wish I had a pair of bongos, bongo fury,' which gave the album its title. Here's an excerpt:

Why, when I was knee-high to a grasshopper,
This black juice came out on a hard-shelled chin.
And they called that 'tobacco juice'.
I used to fiddle with my back feet music for a black onyx.
My entire room absorbed every echo.
The music was ... thud like.
The music was ... thud like.
I usually played such things as rough-neck and thug.
Opaque melodies that would bug most people.
Music from the other side of the fence.

'Poofter's Froth Wyoming Plans Ahead' (Frank Zappa)

Fans disappointed in *Bongo Fury* may point to this track as a stain on its reputation. The music is pretty basic country music (!!!) with Beefheart bawling over the top. Don's vocals are at their harshest, here, as he squeals some pretty high-pitched tones. And I'd be lying if I said Frank and Don are at their best here. As a momentary stop-gap, though, this track serves its purpose and the band seems to be having fun playing this simple track. Watch out for the drum and bass, in particular, as Fowler and Bozzio play around with the rhythm in subtle ways. Don't discount this one just because it's country, especially when it has fun lyrics, including a commentary on the anticipated commercialism of the 1976 bicentennial year:

Poofter's Froth, Wyoming
March Eleven Sixty-Seven
Take a letter,
Ms. Abetter,
An' our pigeons
Will be homing
To our jobbers in Dakota
And to Merwyn, Minnesota
This is merely just a note about
Performance to our quota

'200 Years Old' (Frank Zappa)

A continuation of the bicentennial concept, '200 Years Old' features Beefheart in one of his finest settings: surrounded by thick, greasy, and weird blues. The blues riff plays in G Dorian, with a G-C-Bb-G progression with a countermelody on the synthesizer playing F-C-F#-G. The basic I-IV-I-V-IV-I blues progression is strictly followed, and Beefheart gets the chance to play a nice harmonica solo. As with many blues, the quality of the track is reliant not on the complexity of the music but the feeling in the playing. And Zappa, a lifelong blues fan, plays with plenty. The excellent musicians around him provide a supple background for his solos. And Beefheart sings the mournful melody for all its worth.

'Cucamonga' (Frank Zappa)

'Cucamonga' started as part of 'Farther O'blivion' in live concerts. That track had become a major suite and this segment – which was originally played entirely on brass – must have inspired Zappa, as he removed the music from that context and wrote it some lyrics. It progresses through 2/4, 3/4, and 4/4 segments with ease, as well as multiple modulations. Expect G Lydian, A Mixolydian, and other keys. Chromatic tonalities recur, which was a common Zappa composition trope. The result is a tense atmosphere that feels dissonant while retaining a tonal center.

The rhythm of the melody inspired Zappa's vocal melody, creating odd reads on lines, particularly the Cucamonga line. Lyrically, the song focuses on nostalgia and playing music with friends in the title city. Remember, Frank spent time in this area during the Studio Z days and played in plenty of bands throughout the period.

Note: This track, '200 Years Old,' and a portion of 'Muffin Man' were recorded in the studio.

'Advance Romance' (Frank Zappa)

The lengthiest track on the album is also one of the most complex. It follows a blues-like approach with a 4/4 phrase interrupted by licks in 3/4 and 2/4. The track mostly sits in a G minor scale but ranges into G Dorian, a favored scale for Zappa solos. Napoleon Murphy Brock sings this and navigates the wide vocal with consummate ease. Listen to his deep bass vocals on the 'potato headed Bobby' lyric and how he hits much higher notes on the 'I can't take it no more!' refrain. This type of range was often demanded out of Zappa singers. While he got the easy songs, his singers found themselves ranging from the bottom of their range all the way to the top.

The melody, surprisingly, remains stable and consistent throughout. After Brock explores this theme, Zappa bursts into his first G Dorian solo. Walley supports him with slide guitar as the two create a guitar-lovers paradise before falling into a support role for a one-minute Beefheart harmonica solo. This mini-marvel showcases just how well the Captain could play when asked. Zappa then starts a solo without Walley, continuing in a bluesy vein but throwing in triplets, double-stops, and flurry of notes ala Coltrane's sheets of sound. This solo lasts just under four minutes before Zappa leads the band through two minutes of variations on the main theme. This composed section includes Brock preaching some pretty heavy lyrics before a brief coda.

'Man with the Woman Head' (Don Van Vliet)

The last of the Captain's compositions follows, a 'poem with backing music' approach. And like the first, the music is unnerving and creepy. The lyrics – which sometimes included lines from 'The Torture Never Stops' in some performances – are disturbing in a way I'm sure Burroughs would have approved:

The man with the woman head
Polynesian wallpaper made the face stand out,
A mixture of Oriental and early vaudeville jazz poofter,
Forming a hard, beetle-like, triangular chin much like a praying mantis.

'Muffin Man' (Frank Zappa)

A longtime concert closer, this track combines a studio-based introduction with live sounds. The simple recitation at the beginning is backed by beautiful George Duke keyboard lines. Zappa talks about this titular muffin man before launching into a guitar riff that includes surprising chords, including Daugm-Fugm-G#dim. A walking bass line produces a rock-like style while the band intones:

Girl, you thought he was a man
But he was a muffin
He hung around till you found
That he didn't know nuthin'
Girl, you thought he was a man
But he only was a-puffin'
No cries is heard in the night
As a result of him stuffin'

This gibberish, combined with the melody, creates an ominous atmosphere that is disturbing and hilarious. The track hinges on this theme while Zappa bursts out with an extended and exploratory solo. By this point in his career, just about every solo was either great to mind-blowing, and this multi-scale affair is one for the ages.

Zoot Allures (1976)
Personnel:
Frank Zappa: guitar, bass, lead vocals, synthesizer, keyboards, director of recreational activities
Terry Bozzio: drums, backing vocals
Other Players
Davey Moiré: lead vocals, backing vocals, engineer
Andre Lewis: organ, vocals, backing vocals
Roy Estrada: bass, vocals, backing vocals, drone bass
Napoleon Murphy Brock: vocals
Ruth Underwood: synthesizer, marimba
Captain Beefheart: harmonica
Ruben Ladron de Guevara: backing vocals
Ian Underwood: saxophone
Bruce Fowler: trombone
Sal Marquez: trumpet
Dave Parlato: bass
Lu Ann Neil: harp
Sparky Parker: backing vocals
Producer: Frank Zappa
Recorded Between May-June 1976
Released: October 20, 1976
Peak Chart Position: Number 61 on the Billboard Top 200

By the time 1976 came around, and Zappa's tour with Beefheart had concluded, his backing band was just Terry Bozzio. Everyone else either decided to go on to a solo career – such as George Duke – or, more or less, retired from the industry – like Ruth Underwood. For many bandleaders, such a situation would have been catastrophic. However, just two weeks after the release of *Bongo Fury*, a new Zappa studio album appeared. It had nine tracks and a dark and dreary cover featuring Zappa, Bozzio, Patrick O'Hearn, and Eddie Jobson lounging around like a bunch of sleazy rock and rollers. The music sounds nothing like any produced by Zappa. Slow-paced, ominous, and occasionally simplistic, the album is Zappa's most despairing sounding album.

Was Zappa in despair when the album was recorded? Probably not, though losing his band likely had an emotional effect. However, Frank didn't let setbacks drag him down too long. Instead, he recorded an album almost entirely by himself – O'Hearn and Jobson don't appear on the album at all but would be part of Zappa's next live band. Instead, Zappa plays all the guitar, bass, keyboards, and synthesizers on a vast majority of the studio tracks with Bozzio performing percussion. The sound was occasionally filled out with background singers, and one live track features a small performing combo. A few other players appear, including Ian Underwood, but the sound here is a complete Zappa performance. And the general style is a bluesy and boozy rock sound influenced by metal. Most of the songs are built on riffs with exaggerated simplicity parodying a genre that Zappa found to be quite stupid.

The result is an album that may be hard for some fans to like. At the time, Robert Duncan of *Rolling Stone* praised 'Black Napkins' for its 'uncharacteristically lyrical' solo style and the promisingly dark and moody musical style but trashed Zappa's lyrics as simplistic and meaningless. By contrast, a modern review by François Couture on Allmusic called the album a '... a masterpiece of dark, slow, sleazy rock' and praised it as '...one of Zappa's strongest accomplishments.' As a fan of genial simple music, I have always enjoyed *Zoot Allures*. Sometimes, creating maximum effect with minimal music is much harder to accomplish than with many notes. And though the songs here sometimes ride a single riff and melody to the bitter end, Zappa adds subtle touches,

Note: The original plan for this album was more ambitious than the final result. A test pressing played to *Circus* magazine contained tracks such as 'Sleep Dirt,' 'The Ocean is the Ultimate Solution,' and 'Filthy Habits.' The resulting record would have had a drastically different sound, as these tracks feature more complex and challenging music. The desire for a double album does hint at Zappa's upcoming ambitions and his lengthy legal battles with Warner Brothers over artistic control.

'Wind Up Workin' in a Gas Station' (Frank Zappa)

A good album opener should immediately catch the ear, and this track serves that role well. Starting with a sustained distorted guitar chord, Bozzio bashes for awhile before Zappa starts playing a 4/4 guitar rhythm over Bozzio's animated drumming. The lyrics are another reminder of Zappa's disregard for higher education and more fuel for claims of arrogance or audience disdain that were often levied by his critics:

> Hey now, better make a decision
> Be a moron and keep your position
> You oughta know now all your education
> Won't help you no-how, you're gonna
> Wind up working in a gas station

The lyrics cycle through a few simple phrases, while Frank plays multiple themes. The music changes up to a more sustained style that contrasts with the frantic riffing of the beginning. A brief guitar solo starts the 'show me your thumb if you're really dumb' section, which falls into a 10/16 rhythm. The insane high-pitched falsetto throughout the song is Davey Moire, a man who Zappa used to achieve such effects multiple times throughout his career. He and Zappa sing the tempo and thematic changes with ease, using the stripped-down instrumentation to mask the complexity of the song's arrangement.

'Black Napkins' (Frank Zappa)

One of Zappa's signature guitar pieces, 'Black Napkins' was played at almost every concert until the end of his career. The slow tempo and simplicity of the backing track provide a luxurious launching pad for an extended blues solo. Chords, such as C#m7 and Dmaj7 create a harmonic backing which Zappa explores to its fullest. This live track features Zappa's previous small touring combo (Bozzio, Lewis, Estrada, and Brock) and showcases the tight sound they could achieve. Anyone interested in this period of Zappa's history should listen to 2002's *FZ:OZ*, a full live show by this previously undocumented band. The sharp rock and soul played by this group offers a lot of rewards.

'The Torture Never Stops' (Frank Zappa)

'The Torture Never Stops' is a masterpiece of slow, simple, and gloomy rock. At the time, Zappa was influenced by Alice Cooper (his former disciple) and played tribute – and parody – by slowing the tempo to a funeral dirge and exaggerating the lyrics as much as possible. The result goes beyond mere satire and creates one of the most disturbing atmospheres this side of a Throbbing Gristle album. The incredible thing about this track is that, beyond the drums, Zappa plays all of the instruments. The main musical backing is a bass motif based on a I-VII chord progression in a G Dorian scale. Multiple chords are mixed throughout, including IV and V variations such as Gm, Gsus2, Fsus2, Fadd2, Gm7, and Gsus4. These chords are used to accentuate a harmonically-rich bit of music. And the lyrics? Well, read for yourself:

> *Flies all green 'n buzzin' in his dungeon of despair*
> *Prisoners grumble and piss their clothes and scratch their matted hair*
> *A tiny light from a window hole a hundred yards away*
> *Is all they ever get to know about the regular life in the day*

and

> *Slime 'n rot, rats 'n snot 'n vomit on the floor*
> *Fifty ugly soldiers, man, holdin' spears by the iron door*
> *Knives 'n spikes 'n guns 'n the likes of every tool of pain*
> *An' a sinister midget with a bucket an' a mop where the blood goes down the drain*

This unease is accentuated by lengthy 'tortured' female vocals from an unnamed contributor. These vocals veer into more sexual or orgasmic sounds, which was likely the desired effect. Beyond such sound effects, Zappa keeps the music here minimal and subtle, adding new chords without flash.

Zappa continued to expand upon this track and play it multiple times throughout his career, including the 'more is more' approach of the 1988 band's performance. Though these arrangements utilize horns and synthesizers to create a great sound, no version quite tops this one.

'Ms. Pinky' (Frank Zappa)
Zappa ends side one with one of the silliest tracks on the album. The music is all based on one bass riff (a fine one), and the vocal melody is like Zeppelin's mythical song – it remains the same. The insistence of these themes could drive the listener crazy, but the thicker instrumentation – featuring a guest appearance by Ruth on synth and Vliet on harmonica – keep the track from annoyance. The lyrics center on a blowup sex doll. So not one of Frank's most insightful songs but a fun little diversion. The heavy metal influence makes its most obvious appearance here. And that constant riff, though not among Zappa's most complex musical creations, is still more complex and musically-interesting than most heavy metal riffs of the time.

'Find Her Finer' (Frank Zappa)
Side two opens with another relatively-simple song. The track is driven by a recurring bass riff but, unlike the previous track, the vocal melodies do change. The verses and the choruses differ and feature layered sound effects, background vocals from Roy Estrada, and more Vliet harmonica. The tempo remains rather sedate, and Zappa sings the song as if he is about to fall asleep. Clearly, that was the effect he wanted for a track that features strange romantic advice:

> *Don't never let her know you are smart*
> *The universe is no way to start*
> *You gotta play it straight from the heart*
> *She gwine renunciate you*

Is this a sexist statement claiming that women only love dumb men? Or is it a mockery of such statements? With Frank, the truth is always more complex than it appears. Undoubtedly, he would have claimed it was making fun of the men – not the women – but would have claimed that there was truth to both sides.

'Friendly Little Finger' (Frank Zappa)
By this point, some listeners may be fatigued by the album's endless riffing, no matter how appealing it may sound. Thankfully, 'Friendly Little Finger' provides a different sound at just the right time. The basic track is Frank on guitar and bass, Estrada on 'drone bass,' Bozzio on drums, and Ruth on marimba and synth. Brass is played by Ian Underwood, Bruce Fowler, and Sal Marquez.

The quirky textures focus on an extended guitar solo that features eastern tonalities. The backing music was created using a technique Zappa pioneered known as Xenochrony. The idea was to take one recording and then to place another one recorded separately and without that track's influence directly on top. The accompanying track would then be slightly adjusted. The brief opening theme utilizes 11th chords built on D-E-B-A and G#-A-E-B note combinations. Careful listeners paying attention to the backing tracks will note Zappa plays bass lines that mimic these chords while veering into other tones, such as C-Eb-F#-G-A-B. The track then ends with a brief brass fanfare that somehow feels appropriate.

'Wonderful Wino' (Jeff Simmons, Zappa)

This track originated from the bizarre mind of former Zappa bass player, Jeff Simmons, in 1970. During this year, Simmons and Zappa were working on Jeff's solo album, *Lucille Has Messed My Mind Up,* and Simmons wrote the music for the track but was struggling to come up with lyrics. Zappa suggested he write the lyric, singing from a first-person perspective, on the troubles of alcohol addiction. The resulting lyrics were varied:

> *I went to the country*
> *And while I was gone*
> *I lost control of my body functions*
> *On a roller-headed lady's front lawn*
> *I'm so ashamed, but I'm a wino man*
> *I can't help myself*

After Simmons' album came and went, the song must have stuck in Frank's mind as he re-recorded it for this album. As with most songs here, he recorded the backing tracks alone with Bozzio. The brass was played by Ian Underwood, Bruce Fowler, and Sal Marquez. The result fits in perfectly with the dark and sleazy atmosphere of the rest of the album.

Note: An earlier (and more hard-rocking) version of this song was released on *The Lost Episodes* and featured a possessed Ricky Lancelotti. Some fans may prefer this wilder approach while others may believe that the down-and-out production of this track feels more appropriate for the lyrics.

'Zoot Allures' (Frank Zappa)

'Zoot Allures' is a guitar solo that mixes chords from multiple scales. Frank utilizes G and Dm7 chords in regular progressions that mimic jazz progressions. However, he then builds a thick D# chord around D#-G#-C#-F#-A#, a strange shape that includes three fourths and major thirds. These combinations are utilized on the central theme of the progression, which lasts for nearly three minutes. As always with Frank's solos, the chords change in ways other guitarists or composers in rock wouldn't consider, including using F# and G# chords in a typical V chord and improvised C# Dorian runs over a I-IV progression. Zappa's signature use of triplets late in the solo creates a double-time feel that feels a bit like Charlie Parker at his finest.

'Disco Boy' (Frank Zappa)

Fans wanting Zappa to end the album with a serious track may roll their eyes at 'Disco Boy.' However, this fun rock and roll song not mocks the dance culture of the time but showcases some subtle and clever musicianship. In particularly, Zappa skillfully arranges and overdubs multiple guitar parts and synthesizer sounds to create a unique texture. And the rising bass and drum parts at the end of the verse provide a nice contrast to an otherwise low-key segment. The song also lacks a true chorus. Instead, verses get interrupted by Davey Moire screeching 'DISCO BOOOOOY!!!' at the top of his range. And even if the progression sticks to I-IV-I-IV and a VII-I sound, Frank changes the accents on the chord, switches up the style, and keeps things from getting boring. No matter what one thinks of the lyrics or the basic riff, this song is another fine example of Zappa's ability to make simple songs without being simplistic.

Zappa in New York (1978)
Personnel:
Frank Zappa: conductor, lead guitar, vocals, producer; guitar overdubs
Ray White: rhythm guitar, vocals
Eddie Jobson: keyboards, violin, vocals
Patrick O'Hearn: bass guitar, vocals
Terry Bozzio: drums, vocals
Ruth Underwood: percussion, synthesizer, and various humanly impossible overdubs
Lou Marini: alto sax, flute
Mike Brecker: tenor sax, flute
Ronnie Cuber: baritone sax, clarinet
Randy Brecker: trumpet
Tom Malone: trombone, trumpet, piccolo
Don Pardo: sophisticated narration
David Samuels: timpani, vibes
John Bergamo: percussion overdubs
Ed Mann: percussion overdubs
Lou Anne Neill: osmotic harp overdub
Producer: Frank Zappa
Recorded Between December 26–29, 1976
Released: March 3, 1978
Peak Chart Performance: Number 57 on the Billboard Top 200

Before discussing this album, readers need to understand the rift that had grown between Zappa and Warner Brothers. This strain came to a head when Zappa tried to end his contract with the label by delivering four records at once. Warner refused to pay the advances. This behavior created a lawsuit that ran concurrently with a lawsuit against Herb Cohen and created a legal nightmare. So Frank, stuck in a tough situation, decided to negotiate another contract on his label to release the four albums as a four-record set known as *Lather*. Had it been released, it would have been the first four-record album in rock history. All of these struggles stretched into 1977 when Frank started to press boxes of *Lather* for release. Warner Brothers then suddenly dumped all four of the original albums on the market over a few years without cooperation with Zappa, adding cartoon artwork and with little to no promotion. Their appearance saturated the market and made releasing *Lather* pointless.

Many fans believe that Warner is the villain here. However, Zappa presenting four records at once was an obvious attempt to get out of a contract and somewhat petulant. And Warner understood the dangers of saturating the market with too much material – though later did so anyway. And they likely didn't want to pay Frank advances on so much material or pay to print so many albums at once. Both sides were rather immature and inappropriate and looking at their needs first. As a Zappa fan, I am upset that his music was interfered with in this way but can also understand why Warner acted in such a way. With that important information out of the way, I can discuss this live album, which features a handful of tracks intended for *Lather*.

Recorded at the Palladium in New York City in December of 1976 during four marathon shows, *Zappa in New York* is an excellent example of Zappa's live artistry. There are joke tracks, pop songs, satire, lengthy instrumentals, and reworked golden oldies. Players who stayed with Frank for years after, like Ray White, make their first appearance here. One-time performers, like eternal journeyman Eddie Jobson, also appear. And playing in New York gave Frank the chance to use expert players from the *Saturday Night Live* band. Frank, who performed on the show several times, picked players like Lou Marini, Tom Malone, and the Brecker Brothers for his group. Their added horns opened up his arrangements to include denser and more difficult harmonies. Most amusingly, *SNL* announcer Don Pardo showed up to provide narration. Pardo's madcap sense of humor mixes well with Zappa's and the banter between the two provides welcome levity to an album that is filled with very dense and difficult compositions. The result is a unique sound never heard on other Zappa live albums.

Note: This review focuses on the two-CD version released by Rykodisc and features tracks cut from the original album, bringing the length up to nearly two hours from 70 minutes. A five-disc version of the album was released in 2019, featuring all four shows from which the material was drawn.

'Titties & Beer' (Frank Zappa)
Both the original and expanded album start with this comedy routine between Zappa and Bozzio. The two had a great rapport and are genuinely funny. The music is based on a two-bar F# Dorian riff. Interestingly, the first bar of this phrase is on-beat, while the second is syncopated.

'Cruisin' for Burgers' (Frank Zappa)
The first lengthy instrumental track takes 'Cruisin' for Burgers,' cuts the vocals, and creates pulsing jazz fusion. The introduction adds a bass ostinato that creates a different feel. The themes of the original expand using horn blasts, multiple guitar parts, and thematic development. The rhythmic emphasis throughout the track tweaks multiple times, including 12/16, 3/4, 24/32, 6/8, and even 2/4. There is also a D Mixolydian guitar solo that keeps the track engaging. Fans of the original may not recognize this version as Zappa takes advantage of the expanded band format.

'I Promise Not to Come in Your Mouth' (Frank Zappa)
This indelicately-titled track is a surprisingly sensitive track that uses a 6/4 rhythm in a key rarely used by Zappa: C minor. Sustained melodies over the first several bars create intrigue while a chord progression of Dm-F-G-Dm-G-Eb-Ebmaj7 provides appropriate backing for keyboard improvisations. Zappa then

plays a guitar solo that starts in D Lydian but which progresses to C# Lydian and F# Dorian before Eddie Jobson takes a keyboard solo. Jobson plays in Bb Dorian, C Lydian, C Dorian, C# Lydian, Eb Mixolydian, D Mixolydian, and more. The backing tracks remain supple.

'Punky's Whips' (Frank Zappa)

Warner Brothers hated this track and recalled the first release to eliminate it. The lyrical theme – as sung by Terry Bozzio – is a bit much, though the simulated passion for Punky is compelling. More interesting is the music, which goes through several themes, rhythms, and tempos. Anticipate 14/32, 17/32, 18/32, and 33/32 bars throughout this track. Chords expand to include ninth progressions, Ab notes, and excellent horn arrangements. The closing segment heralded by excellent Bozzio percussion is one of the best bits of music on the album.

'Honey, Don't You Want a Man Like Me?' (Frank Zappa)

A simple pop song often used as an example of Zappa's sexism. The woman described in the song is, clearly, not someone Zappa likes:

> *She was a lonely sort, just a little too short*
> *Her jokes were dumb and her fav'rite sport*
> *Was hockey (in the winter)*

However, the guy in the song is by no means presented as a gentleman:

> *He was the Playboy Type (he smoked a pipe)*
> *His fav'rite phrase was 'OUTA-SITE!'*
> *He had an Irish Setter'*

and:

> *He called her a slut*
> *A pig and a whore*
> *A bitch and a cunt*
> *And she slammed the door*

So is the song sexist or a realistic example of the 'single bar' dating lifestyle? That probably varies depending on the listener. And while there are multiple versions of this track available on several albums, the basic structure stays about the same.

'The Illinois Enema Bandit' (Frank Zappa)

The first appearance of *SNL* announcer Don Pardo, this track is a lengthy blues sung wonderfully by Ray White. White's blues voice was always appropriately utilized by Zappa whenever he got the chance. Pardo announces the song with his amusing vocal tone, adding a little bit of humor. The song itself is fairly simple and mostly lyrics-based, as the band sings about the exploits of Michael Kenyon, a young man who robbed women and then gave them an enema. Is this sexist? In this instance, I feel confident saying that it isn't. Frank is singing about a strange occurrence and reporting the details of the situation. It mostly sticks to a blues-based structure and melodies, giving Zappa the chance to showcase his advanced blues soloing. The oddest moment comes at the end when they start chanting in tribute to Roy Estrada. Estrada would later appear on stage as the enema bandit in later tours.

'I'm the Slime' (Frank Zappa)
The second disc of the album starts with an excellent reading of this track. The expanded horn introduction provides more harmonic depth. Verses are backed not by the bass and clavinet of the original recording but by Jobson synthesizer chords. The highlight is Pardo's hilarious reading of the 'You will obey me while I lead you' segment.

'Pound for a Brown' (Frank Zappa)
'Pound for a Brown' feels very similar to 'Cruisin' for Burgers,' as the sturdy melodies of both pieces highlight how strong Zappa's writing was early in his life, as both were written as string quartets when he was a teen. Meters include 3/4 and 4/4 played over an ostinato written for the new arrangement.

'Manx Needs Women' (Frank Zappa)
Though this track is brief, Zappa packs it with a large amount of content. For example, there are major seventh chords, 4/4 bars, 7/16 rhythms, and atonal accents that create an aggressive and harsh tone. There are even 11-tuplet (!!!) segments used as casually as most composers use blues chord progressions.

'The Black Page Drum Solo/Black Page #1' (Frank Zappa)
This piece of music was written by Zappa to weed out weak drummers and to get only the best for his band. The title comes from the fact that the sheet music was filled with so many notes that it looked like a 'black page.' Multiple versions of this song are available, though this was the first released.

The original drum solo is played using a 4/4 meter, and the flurry of notes bashed out by Bozzio are dizzying but flawlessly executed. The second part of the instrumental is a full-band version that uses multiple scales, triplets, quintuplets, and scales like G Lydian, Bb Lydian, D Lydian, and Gb Lydian.

'Big Leg Emma' (Frank Zappa)
After such a staggeringly-difficult piece, the band likely enjoyed relaxing with this pop song. The extra horns add a brassy sound unique from the original.

Zappa's understanding of concert pacing was superlative, as he would often utilize such contrasts to avoid audience fatigue.

'Sofa' (Frank Zappa)
This version of 'Sofa' is one of the finest instrumental renditions of this tune available. Zappa takes full advantage of the extra horns to transform this through-composed melody into a jazz symphony punctuated by keyboard textures and guitar punctuation. The slowed tempo creates an almost R&B feel that differentiates it from other versions. Coming after the silliness of 'Big Leg Emma, 'Sofa' provides a little musical meat. Listen to those flute lines at about 2:00 to grasp how fully Zappa understood the benefits of his expanded lineup and how to write arrangements to take advantage of the extra sonic possibilities.

'Black Page #2' (Frank Zappa)
Taking the basic rhythmic backing from 'Black Page #1,' Zappa composed a melody over the top to make it easier for the audience. This particular version is a bit slower than others, which gives the listener the chance to dig into a strange but appealing melody. Zappa would state that this was the 'dance' version of the song and claims in the lengthy introduction that it is 'disco.' He would then have a dance contest during this track, which caused amusingly confused and sporadic movements from stoned audience members.

'The Torture Never Stops' (Frank Zappa)
The first expanded version of this track isn't as densely arranged as the 1988 take, but offers a few differences from the studio recording. Flutes accentuate the introduction to expand the melody, and the keyboard lines provide extra flourish when compared to Zappa's relatively simple playing. O'Hearn on bass is particularly effective, as he adds melodic tweaks that stay within the basic harmony and melodic style. The expanded percussion make the track feel more alive and open. Zappa then plays a focused and effective solo that mournfully compliments the mood.

'The Purple Lagoon/Approximate' (Frank Zappa)
Though Frank had (mostly) given up on dense and expansive jazz fusion tracks after *The Grand Wazoo*, he occasionally returned to the format. 'The Purple Lagoon' is one of these tracks, a dense and unpredictable composition that very rarely gets the attention that it deserves. The frantic opening showcases incredible O'Hearn bass work. Frank again uses the extra horns to utilize a very dense sheet of brass sound. The textures created on this track create harmonies you can't find anywhere else in his catalog – and frankly, in very little in jazz or rock music. As multiple themes are explored throughout, solos pop in and out and create a constantly shifting and grooving piece of music.

The track comes to a shocking end when Frank gets his huge band to play 'Approximate,' a tune that features rhythm notation but no notes, meaning that every member plays whatever melody they want to the rhythm track. The result is a stomping ending to a dazzling piece and a superlative end to one of Frank's best live albums.

Studio Tan (1978)

Personnel:
Frank Zappa: guitar, vocals, percussion
Davey Moire: vocals
George Duke: keyboards
Eddie Jobson: keyboards & yodeling
Tom Fowler: bass guitar
Max Bennett: bass guitar
James 'Bird Legs' Youman: bass guitar
Chester Thompson: drums
Paul Humphrey: drums
Don Brewer: bongos
Ruth Underwood: percussion & synthesizer
Producer: Frank Zappa
Recorded in 1969 and 1974–1976
Released: September 15, 1978
Peak Chart Position: Number 147 on the Billboard Top 200

Though the legal wrangling that surrounded the *Lather* fiasco deserves an entire book, this is not an examination of legal and sociological issues. We're here to talk about the music – which is ultimately the most important element anyway – so let's move on to the first studio project of *Lather* material.

Studio Tan contained four tracks, each of which showcases a different side of the project. 'Let Me Take You To The Beach' is a silly – but complex – pop song; 'Revised Music for Guitar & Low-Budget Guitar' are intensive instrumentals with jazz and classical elements; and 'The Adventures of Greggery Peccary' is a 20-minute classical avant-guard piece turned into a cartoon soundtrack. The music here is wildly diverse and densely composed and shows Frank moving in even more difficult directions in rock. Though moments of simplicity appear, he was attempting to produce serious music that pushed the boundaries of not only composition and playing in rock bands but – for better or worse – common sense and good taste. And, in a single sentence, that's why *Lather* is so awesome.

Unfortunately, *Studio Tan* did not continue Frank's chart successes in the decade and fell outside the Top 100. Part of this was due to the difficulty of the music but also poor promotion by Warners. The silly cartoon cover – which does have its charms – likely did little to help its sales. As a result, reviews at the time were minimal: Robert Christgau only mentioned the album – insultingly – in passing in a positive *Sleep Dirt* review. However, modern reviews appraise the album as a fine piece of work. 'Ultimate Classic Rock' states that 'Despite the artist's misgivings about the edited state in which it was presented, Studio Tan harbors plenty of engaging examples of Zappa's wide-ranging musical brilliance.' Allmusic.com praised 'Greggery Peccary' stating: 'Yet, it is greater than the sum of its parts, proposing an unmatched musical narrative that makes 'Billy the Mountain' the work of a child and amounts to a stunning synthesis of the man's influences, stylistic range, and studio techniques.' They commented, briefly, on 'Revised Music' and 'RDZNL,' stating that they were fine instrumental tracks.

'The Adventures of Greggery Peccary' (Frank Zappa)

When playing this track to a friend, I was disappointed – but not surprised – to hear him say that it was 'a bit much.' Another friend – a huge Zappa nut – was also ambivalent about the track and seemed to have similar misgivings about its complexity, preferring the more streamlined 'Billy the Mountain.' Dropping the veil of objectivity, I think that 'Greggery' is a masterpiece and one of Frank's best pieces of music – an opinion the writer shares with the composer. Frank's continued interest in combining music and literature – which started as early as 1964 – reaches a peak to never again be topped – perhaps only on *Joe's Garage*. The fact that this music had been brewing in his head as early as 1970 and '71 shows how important he considered the track. The recording took three years and required an army of musicians. What really sets this piece apart is the unique construction. Rather than the leitmotif approach of 'Billy,' 'Greggery Peccary' is 25 pieces of music strung together in a coherent and engaging manner.

Breaking down the track into all of its components would likely require a book and an advanced musical degree. Suffice to say that the tempos, time signatures, and scales change constantly and create a baffling, but unappealing, barrage. Expect atonality over 7/8 time signatures, 10/8 and 6/8 vamps, and dense chromatic passages. Two moments that always stand out for me: the moment when the music stops and Greggery asks 'What?' as if commenting on the music always makes me laugh out loud. And the sudden jump into the simplicity and unadorned beauty of the 'New Brown Clouds' theme is nearly on par with the 'Ode to Joy' choral reveal in Beethoven's Ninth: I'm absolutely serious.

The lyrics here go far beyond the funny – but sometimes juvenile – style of 'Billy the Mountain' and satirize the fear of growing old common in all people but, in particular, Zappa's generation of 'slowly aging' hippies. While the music here is dense, the 'over the top' approach is flawlessly executed.

Note: The original *Lather* album ends with 'The Adventures of Greggery Peccary', and that seems like a better place for it than album opener. Though the rest of the tracks on this album are among Frank's finest of the period, it's hard not to feel like Greggery overwhelms them.

'Music for Low-Budget Orchestra' (Frank Zappa)

Although this piece was originally recorded as early as *Lumpy Gravy*, its definitive recording didn't come until 1974-75. A version is available on *Jean-Luc Ponty Plays the Music of Frank Zappa*, though this version is definitive. The 'low budget' orchestra is a classical ensemble mixed with Frank's '75-era band, including George Duke, Bruce, and Tom Fowler, and Chester Thompson. The opening is low key, and the main melody taken up mostly by Frank's guitar. The first 14 bars move through extended chords and several keys, including Bb Mixolydian, Bm, C Mixolydian, C#m, and D Phrygian. Chords such as Bb13, B11, C13, C#m7add6, and D+7(b9) create a rather dense and nearly atonal feel enhanced by Duke's piano. Changes to more horn- and flute-based melodies create a pleasant contrast with the more lackadaisical beginning, particularly when the oboe, violin, and more start playing melodies that dance playfully. The density of the writing continues to expand, with Frank's acoustic guitar playing melodies expanded on by the piano and orchestra.

The music may lack the rock-based sound of *Hot Rats* or the jazzier feel of the *Wazoo*-era albums, but the mixture of rock instruments playing over dense orchestral textures is unique. This is a Zappa more concentrated on classical music and tightly-composed passages. Not a track you whistle-along to, then, but one that you can listen to with your eyes closed.

'Lemme Take You To The Beach' (Frank Zappa)

And now for something completely different! Zappa goes surf pop with the fast-paced keyboard passages adding a bit of pizzazz. The opening phrase is a simple I-II chord progression in an A Dorian scale. Eddie Jobson plays these keyboards in one of his few studio performances for Zappa. The lyrics are intentionally stupid and sung by Davey Moire at his adenoidal finest. Though the song is under three minutes, Frank clearly took the composition of such a silly little 'throwaway' piece quite seriously. In the first minute, you get three themes, including multiple modulations.

For example, the first sung theme uses the now non-arpeggiated chords from the intro as a backing. The sung melody jumps up a fourth while the chords switch to a IV-II progression. Then, the second theme comes into play, modulated to a C with the bass following a I-VI-II-V progression. After a shift to E Mixolydian on the same theme – and a repetition of theme one – the third theme appears, including a C-Ab-G-C progression before the first theme appears as an instrumental. To avoid boring the reader too much (too late!), suffice to say that the song features extensive attention to detail. Beyond these modulations and tempo shifts lie the bursts of keyboard from Jobson and the pleasant, organ-led instrumental bridge. This may be one of the finest pop tracks of Zappa's '70s career.

'RDNZL' (Frank Zappa)

'RDNZL' – or 'Redunzl' – was written in 1972 and versions exist on *The Lost Episodes* compilation and on the second volume of the *You Can't Do That On Stage Anymore* series. These early versions are sketches compared to this unstoppable instrumental showcase. Fans of Zappa's most complex rock-based work will find a lot to love here, though – like 'Music for Low-

Budget Orchestra' – they won't walk away singing the instrumental melodies. The opening instrumental sets the mood right away, containing the kind of pounding instrumental intensity and scale flourishes that only Zappa – in the rock world – used. After this intense opening, a low-key melody plays over bass and Ruth Underwood's percussion. Piano improvisations make brief interruptions in the melody, which continues to be expanded with synthesizer and percussion sounds.

These variations continue until Zappa starts playing an attractive solo. George Duke's piano is particularly important, comping, adding more elaborate chords and almost boogie-woogie style runs and being the musical foil that Frank deserved. Chester Thompson and James Youmans on drums and bass, respectively, create a propulsive backing filled with interjections and reactions. The solo ends with more intense and darker-tinged textures. As bass, piano, and drums delve into dark areas, the track varies these melodies for a few seconds until an almost silly synthesizer theme appears. With its mock-heroic tone, the natural reaction is to laugh, and Frank would have appreciated the reaction as it's undoubtedly the effect he hoped to achieve.

After a burst of percussion from Ruth and Chester and a nearly bluesy melody, a piano-based comp drives the rest of the track. The simple keyboard chords provide a nice change, as Youmans and Chester lock into a tight groove to back another Duke piano solo. The man never played poorly and fans of his work will appreciate this showcase. Duke ends his solo with dense clusters of notes that simulate the feel of a dark horror movie soundtrack before more percussion and synthesizer bursts set up blindingly fast synthesizer arpeggios and the kind of drumming that makes Chester Thompson a legend. The melody of the opening comes back in at a slower tempo to bring the piece to a close.

Sleep Dirt (1979)

Personnel:
Frank Zappa: guitar, percussion, keyboards, synthesizer
Patrick O'Hearn: bass guitar
Terry Bozzio: drums
George Duke: keyboards, vocals
Bruce Fowler: brass
Dave Parlato: bass guitar
Chester Thompson: drums
Ruth Underwood: percussion, keyboards
James 'Bird Legs' Youman: bass guitar, rhythm guitar
Thana Harris: vocals (CD remix)
Chad Wackerman: drum overdubs (CD remix)
Recorded between December 5–26, 1974 and 1976
Released: January 19, 1979
Producer: Frank Zappa
Peak Chart Position: Number 175 on the Billboard Top 200

Continuing the trend set by *Studio Tan*, *Sleep Dirt* includes an album cover not approved of by Frank and was one of his lowest charting positions: the album barely made the charts, which was due to Warners' indifference to promoting it. At the time, Frank wanted to call the album *Hot Rats III* but was not allowed by Warners, perhaps because their relationship had gotten so poor they didn't want to do anything Zappa suggested.

At the time, it was Frank's first completely instrumental album and featured some of his most serious and twisted music. Critics at the time praised it, with Robert Christgau saying it was Frank's best album in years while snidely suggesting it was because Frank didn't sing on it. Much of the material on the album was intended for a musical, *Hutchentoot*, including 'Flambay,' 'Spider of Destiny,' and 'Time is Money.' On the original release, the intended lyrics for these tracks weren't added but Zappa later added vocals by Thana Harris in 1991 and had Chad Wackerman overdub new drum tracks. The 2012 release removes these overdubs.

Are the songs better with lyrics or do they work better as instrumentals? That depends on taste, but I tend to prefer the instrumentals. Fans of the original may also appreciate the vocal-free versions. Objectively speaking, though, the vocals add structure to the tracks and Harris' singing is unique to Zappa's oeuvre and worth hearing. Modern reviews praise the album, with 'Ultimate Classic Rock' claiming that the title track is 'one of Zappa's best instrumentals from the period.' Allmusic was more ambivalent, saying the album was 'musical fragments.'

'Filthy Habits' (Frank Zappa)

'Filthy Habits' is a strange way to start. Originally part of the aborted double album *Night of The Iron Sausage* that later became the single *Zoot Allures*, this track is a guitar piece unlike anything else Frank ever released. It features harmonized feedback, stomping bass, rock drumming, and sustained notes that produce an imposing sound later arranged with horns and in an expansive instrumental.

Most of the piece has a vamp-based backing that allows Frank to solo effectively. The 5/4 rhythmic backing is unusual but adds to the uneasiness. Frank plays a melismatic melody through many Eastern-tinged scales, including Fm and F Phrygian alterations. Fans of Zappa's guitar work will find a lot to love here, as he continually overdubs himself over Dave Parlato and Terrio Bozzio's bass and drums. In fact, I think it's nearly Frank's best guitar exploration if not for the last track on this album. These two tracks alone justify the purchase of this album, as Frank does things on guitar here that he never approached again later.

'Flambe' (Frank Zappa)

The opening piano showcases George Duke in an unusual lounge-style setting. This song parodies the standard 'Laura,' and features great Duke keys. Other players include Patrick O'Hearn on string bass, Chester Thompson on drums, and Ruth Underwood on percussion. The 1991 CD has Wackerman on drums. Replacing Chester Thompson on drums? Madness.

Though the original version was completely instrumental, the music is less outrageous than *Studio Tan*. That said, the relaxed melody is very fine, and one doesn't need the vocals to appreciate the changes in tonality and instrumentation. Underwood, in particular, is critical for shaping the melody with her inventive percussion parts. Duke gets a great piano solo at just under two minutes that stays within the established tempo' to produce a homogeneous whole different than Zappa instrumentals that tend to veer from one idea to the next. Fans expecting that kind of approach here may be disappointed, but the mood is nice.

Do the added vocals help or hinder the enjoyment of this piece? Harris' fine singing provides a surprisingly beautiful rendering of some rather silly lyrics, including lines like 'He wasn't smart, he wasn't handsome either, but he thrilled me when he drilled me.' Contrasting a serious singing approach with ridiculous lyrics was a common Zappa trope and Harris does it fine here.

'Spider of Destiny' (Frank Zappa)

Compared to the sedate atmosphere created on the previous track, 'Spider of Destiny' is more upbeat. Frank's guitar plays the whole-tone melody that Harris will later mirror. This approach was by design, undoubtedly, and produces a pleasant effect, though it must be said that individuals coming to the sung version from the instrumental may find the effect jarring. That has nothing to do with Harris, as she continues to do a beautiful job giving real weight to the silly lyrics. Hearing a great singer perform lyrics like 'Listen carefully, spider of destiny, you must heed the call of cosmo-biology, listen to me!' is much funnier than hearing Zappa sing them. Frank could only have emphasized their ridiculousness rather than rendered them sublime.

The main theme – stated by Zappa on guitar – is repeated twice before the second theme briefly appears. The third theme comes before a repeat of the main theme pops up and stays until the end of the track. Duke, Underwood, O'Hearn, Thompson play off of each other beautifully and create some staggeringly complex harmonic work for what appears to be a fairly straight forward track – another example of Zappa's subtle composition excellence.

'Regyptian Strut' (Frank Zappa)

Stuffed into the middle of an album, 'Regyptian Strut' feels somewhat out of place. The pomp and circumstance of the track feel more natural as an album opener, which is where it fits on *Lather*. However, the placement here doesn't detract from the musical quality. There's a universal appeal to this composition: my father, an avowed George Jones fan, quite liked this one.

The march-based rhythm features horn melodies that feel parodic or satiric when paired with Ruth's excellent percussion. It's hard not to feel like Frank was having fun composing in a focused format and making fun of the style while also adding a high level of composition sophistication. The bass lines provide beautiful counterpoint movements to the main melodies and harmonies. Expect changes C Lydian and the addition of chords like the Bbadd2 over the vamp. As the melody gets reprised, the harmonies expand, with Esus2 chords and a multitude of variations. When the stately second theme occurs, the scales stabilize with wonderful horn interjections to add more grandeur. Subtle changes, such as parallel fourths and thirds and an overdubbed brass section playing an octave high, create a piece of music that would work beautifully as a national anthem.

'Time is Money' (Frank Zappa)

A return to the jazzy style of 'Flambe' 'Time is More' throws in Zappa-style flourishes. The guitar playing is more complex than on 'Flambe' and features interjections typical for Frank's composition style. Lots of unison notes between the guitar, bass, and percussion highlight a complex melody that Harris handles with shocking ease.

Chords expand from basic triads to more complex ones at the drop of a hat, and the synthesizers are used liberally to produce jarring and dark textures. Anticipate changes from 4/4 to 3/4 time signatures dropped in without a moment's notice and an array of moods that Harris helps to define with lyrics like:

Time is money, space is a long, long time!
On my lonely throne, in the cosmic night
I ponder the vast expanses between

your puny world and mine!

I'd say that this track is the one that most benefits from the singing. Harris provides a structure that the average listener can catch more easily when listening to the dense complexities of the instrumental.

'Sleep Dirt' (Frank Zappa)

The acoustic duet between Frank and James Youmans is something rarely heard from Zappa. Youmans plays the rhythmic chord progression over which Frank solos. The bluesier style pairs wonderfully with the jazzy-style chords Youmans expands upon as he plays. Pieces like these put the lie to the criticism that Zappa was incapable of emotional playing. The sharp stinging lines are filled with feeling, and the chord progression is rich and varied. This track serves as a great intro to the final track, which may be Zappa's finest moment as a guitarist.

'The Ocean is the Ultimate Solution' (Frank Zappa)

Over the years, Frank's guitar technique had increased to such a point that he was one of the finest soloists of his generation. There's a reason why he started releasing albums that featured nothing but his solos: they had gone from mere interjections to become compositions in and of themselves. And no track really showcases that quite like this one.

Note: The original version of this track is over 13 minutes long, but the version on *Lather* cuts off the first five minutes. This change forced me to buy *Sleep Dirt*. The edited version does start at the moment that track really starts blazing, but the exploratory material before that point is sadly missed. The original version of this song was a half-hour jam with Zappa, O'Hearn (string and electric bass) and Terry Bozzio (drums). The improvised music was special, but Frank knew that the original version was too long. So he pulled 13 minutes from the track and edited them together, overdubbed some brief synthesizer lines and guitar soloing, and created a masterpiece.

The starting melody, played on synth and bass, is almost comical and sorely missed on the *Lather* re-re-release. Frank comes in on guitar backed by Terry's animated drumming and O'Hearn''s frantic bass playing. Zappa's guitar chords stick to a C Mixolydian progression backed by the psychic playing of O'Hearn. Frank adds some fast synthesizer to add a bit more depth while Bozzio propels the two soloists forwards. Frank and O'Hearn play chromatic scales, D-based scales, A Dorian, F Dorian, F Mixolydian, and C Mixolydian throughout the first five minutes that produce a harmonic richness shocking in an improv-based environment. The interplay between Zappa and O'Hearn is one of the best Frank possessed with any bass player in his band.

When the later version starts, Frank plays a great riff and an array of notes in an Eastern-tinged scale. O'Hearn starts a solo that bucks the trend of boring bass solos by being fast, engaging, and varied in its melodic approach. O'Hearn is smart and avoids deep notes to play higher runs. Zappa and Bozzio come in on support as O'Hearn continues to explore variations of themes stated earlier in the solo. At one point he bums a note and grunts 'damn it!' which is, amusingly, credited as lyrics. Frank then overdubs himself on electric guitar and plays through Dorian and Mixolydian scales over Bb, F, and C pedal notes on the best solo of his career.

Such a statement is grand and very subjective, but the way Frank plays off of O'Hearn and Bozzio (and himself) is unreal. The drama he creates is amazing, particularly the way he reacts to musicians playing at a different session. His soloing is clever enough to not only react to what the other musicians are doing but to make it feel as if they are reacting to his playing at the same time.

The effect includes a flurry of notes, licks, and high-pitched shrieks that shape the air in a way I'm not sure Frank touched before or after. Again, his work here is not mere showing off – as Christgau and other critics at the time misunderstood – but spontaneous composition of the highest level in rock.

Sheik Yerbouti (1979)

Personnel:
Frank Zappa: lead guitar, lead and backing vocals, arranger, composer, producer, remixing
Davey Moire: lead and backing vocals, engineer
Napoleon Murphy Brock: lead and backing vocals
Andre Lewis: backing vocals
Randy Thornton: lead and backing vocals
Adrian Belew: rhythm guitar, lead and backing vocals, Bob Dylan impersonation
Tommy Mars: keyboards, backing and lead vocals
Peter Wolf: keyboards, butter, Flora margarine
Patrick O'Hearn: bass, lead and backing vocals
Terry Bozzio: drums, lead and backing vocals
Ed Mann: percussion, backing vocals
David Ocker: clarinet
Producer: Frank Zappa
Recorded on January 25–27, February 28, 1978, and October 30–31, 1977
Released: March 3, 1979
Peak Chart Performance: Number 4 on Swedish Album Charts, Number 5 on Norwegian Album Charts, Number 6 on Austrian Album Charts, Number 10 on the German Album Charts, Number 21 on Dutch and US Billboard Charts, Number 32 on the UK Album Charts, and Number 36 on New Zealand Album Charts

After the *Lather* fiasco, Frank needed to recapture the interest of his audience to stay relevant. To meet this end, his first release on his eponymous label, the double *Sheik Yerbouti*, not only reaffirmed Frank's commercial clout but, surprisingly, improved his critical standing. For example, *Rolling Stone*'s David Fricke was positive about the album, stating '(The album) reaffirms (at least for the faithful) Zappa's chops as a bandleader and rock & roll wit who doesn't have to be socially relevant to get a laugh.' He also praises the album as a 'refreshingly straightforward record' while praising 'Flakes' and 'City of Tiny Lites' and Zappa's guitar playing on 'Yo Mama.' He ends the review stating that '(*Sheik Yerbouti*) offers proof that, ten years after his supposed heyday, this sheik can still shake it.'

However, Robert Christgau gave it a C and stated that it 'Makes you wonder whether his primo guitar solo on 'Yo' Mama' and those as-unique-as-they-used-to-be rhythms and textures are as arid spiritually as he is. As if there were any question after all these years,' his main problem being what he perceived as Zappa's satirical attacks on what Christgau called normal people. Though I often find Christgau is off-point, I sort of agree with this idea: Zappa's satire is sometimes a bit off on this album. The broader focus on cultural morays has become more focused on individuals. He mocks jocks ('Bobby Brown'), races ('Jewish Princess'), and unionized laborers ('Flakes'). Though these are relevant topics, they feel like the infamous 'Old Man Yells at

Cloud' headline in *The Simpsons*. At the same time, satire need not be broad to be effective. People like Bobby Brown do exist, which is why when the Anti-Defamation League demanded an apology for 'Jewish Princess,' Frank refused saying 'Unlike the unicorn, such creatures do exist—and deserve to be 'commemorated' with their own special opus.'

Lyrics aside, the music is an interesting change for Frank. Mostly recorded live, the backing tracks were taken into the studio for overdubs using xenochrony. This technique found Frank stacking unrelated performances to create a unique mix that would never have otherwise existed. A handful of tracks here feature this approach. And most of the tracks segue into each other in a rapid-fire manner: another example of Frank's skilled editing expertise.

In spite of such cutting-edge mixing, the music is Frank's simplest and most focused yet. Jazz, classical, music concrete, and other adventurous styles are mostly jettisoned in favor of rock songs. The simpler approach opened him up to a wider audience, many of whom undoubtedly went back to past albums to explore his catalog more extensively. I was one of them: after trying several albums that I couldn't yet understand at that point in my musical journey, *Sheik Yerbouti* hit me hard and inspired me to check out more complex music. Most importantly, the album does work as a diverse, entertaining, and well-written rock album. Every song has a tight melody, a catchy riff, and superlative arrangements. Although time signature and tempo changes remain minimal, many scales, melodic approaches, and genre styles are mixed together in Zappa's emulation of *The White Album*, though Frank's band tends to create a more uniform sound than that Beatles' masterpiece – my favorite of theirs. Fans of this era are encouraged to listen to the *Hammersmith Odeon* live collection, which features undoctored versions of the songs here.

'I Have Been In You' (Frank Zappa)

Frank starts with what can almost be called a romantic soul ballad. Though the song lacks the explanation found in live shows – i.e., a mockery of the ridiculousness of Peter Frampton's album and song title, 'I'm In You' – the lyrics remain funny, and the backing music has a subtlety that makes it more interesting than the average soul ballad.

'Flakes' (Frank Zappa)

'Flakes' is a mini-prog epic with at least three themes in each version, a Bob Dylan impersonation by Adrian Belew, a snappy prog riff, brief instrumental passages with a bit of improvisation, an amusing section discussing the failure of repair technicians, and a surprising outro that gives the track a grand feel.

'Broken Hearts Are For Assholes' (Frank Zappa)

Frank had little time for punk rock, and this emulation has a simple riff that is something Frank could have written in his sleep, but the energetic performances (and Bozzio's vocal interjections) make the track entertaining.

During the lengthy slow-paced bridge section, O'Hearn's descriptive lyrical improvisations are both amusing and disgusting.

'I'm So Cute' (Frank Zappa)
This punk-style track features Terry Bozzio preaching it with screams of '1, 2, 3, 4!' (Bozzio's tribute to the Ramones). A sold guitar riff moves into an organ-based variation that includes Davey Moire's unmistakable falsetto. Although the components here are pretty simple, Frank varies them with surprising fluidity to create a song that is never boring.

'Jones Crusher' (Frank Zappa)
The first track on the second side is a bluesier track, with Frank and Adrian Below getting into some excellent guitar interplay. Belew shows off the guitar work he'd put to great use with David Bowie, King Crimson, and Nine Inch Nails. His vocal work adds a little diversity to the album sometimes missing on some earlier albums. Having better singers allowed more approaches than when Frank, with his appealing but limited vocalization, handled all vocals. The track features basic musical ideas quickly varied to create a dazzling effect that keeps veteran listeners more engaged and new listeners entertained.

'Whatever Happened to All the Fun in the World?' (Frank Zappa)
A 35-second burst of editing featuring new jokes and stuff recorded from the *Lumpy Gravy* sessions. Though hardly a major work, it does add a little diversity to the album's more rock-based style.

'Rat Tomango' (Frank Zappa)
This five-minute solo was pulled from 'The Torture Never Stops.' Though by no means his finest solo, it's worth a listen because Frank Zappa was an engaging music statement.

'We've Got to Get into Something Real' (Frank Zappa)
This is a bit of music concrete that features an unidentified performance on which Terry Bozzio complains about Zappa. It's kind of amusing.

'Bobby Brown' (Frank Zappa)
Another 'soul' style ballad, 'Bobby Brown' is one of Frank's most controversial tracks. Some state that the song is sexist, but the titular character's toxic masculinity is the real point of the song. The women attacking him are not painted as villains but as heroes, of a sort. Oddly, this track was very popular in parts of Europe, and Zappa wanted to hire an anthropologist to understand why it was a huge hit.

'Rubber Shirt' (Frank Zappa)
'Rubber Shirt' is the biggest example of xenochrony on the album. O'Hearn plays a bass improv completely unrelated to Terry Bozzio's drum part. The end effect is a rather slow-motion dance between two musicians who never heard the other player's part.

'Sheik Yerbouti Tango' (Frank Zappa)
This track, one of only a handful of tango tracks released by Frank, is a solo nicked from a live version of 'Little House I Used to Live In.' The keyboard backing features some fine piano and quite a bit of Tommy Mars' infamous synth tones. A little organ helps provide a richer harmonic bed for the solo.

'Baby Snakes' (Frank Zappa)
The second record starts with this just-under-two-minute track that surprisingly has four unique themes. The first theme starts with the 'baby snake' vocalization before a second theme appears at 41 seconds and a third at 1:01 before the first theme reprises itself in the coda: compact, diverse, and effective pop songwriting.

'Trying to Grow a Chin' (Frank Zappa)
This track is a heavy rocker that features Bozzio at his finest. At this point, the young Bozzio had become a legend in Frank's circle. His constant energy, impeccable timing, and bizarre sense of humor made him the perfect foil for Zappa. With slightly more complex arrangements – including great percussion work by Ed Mann – this mini-opera features Bozzio's best vocal performance.

'City of Tiny Lites' (Frank Zappa)
As an Adrian Below vocal showcase, this track is gorgeous. The piano, bass, organ, and percussion arrangement produces an epic feel. It features quite a number of side riffs, alternate sections, and a multitude of synth overdubs that produce an unpredictable style.

'Dancin' Fool' (Frank Zappa)
Frank's second parody of disco was, ironically, a big hit in the dance clubs. Understandably: the song is catchy and has an authentic disco beat. The percussion overdubs add the necessary Zappa element, as do the weird synthesizer effects. Ironically, this track was a huge hit in discos – in spite of the character assassination of disco dancers. In fact, it was nominated for a Grammy: Frank's first nomination, though he didn't win. When he did win – in 1988 for *Jazz From Hell* – he did not accept the award, claiming that award shows were 'fake.' He won two more Grammys: 1996's 'Boxed or Special Limited Edition 'award for *Civilization Phaze III* and a 1997 'Lifetime Achievement' award.

'Jewish Princess' (Frank Zappa)
The percussion and kazoo opening of this track let you know you're in for something silly. The instrumental textures include percussion, synth, piano, bass, organ, vocal overdubs, and a multitude of other sounds. The lyrics... well, I can understand why the Anti-Defamation League didn't like this song. That said, the music remains a fine example of Zappa's pop songwriting.

'Wild Love' (Frank Zappa)
The last side of the album starts with an excellent guitar melody with an epic feel that makes it a bit more engaging than earlier tracks. Frank varies from the straighter composition styles showcased earlier, using a multitude of eighth and sixteenth notes for his melodies. Each segment of the track goes through multiple sections with various singers intoning their dedication to 'wild love.' Though the verses follow the same structure, they remain varied and engaging. The result is a mini-epic that sets the listener up for the ending track.

'Yo Mama' (Frank Zappa)
Fans wanting Zappa guitar soloing get plenty here. The opening moments contain a unique sense of space not common on this album. The gorgeous percussion and organs back harmonized vocals to produce a pleasant effect. The lyrics are very scathing but hardly the main point of the song. The solo starts at 1:57 after a brief flurry of keyboards. This band had two keyboard players (Peter Wolf and Tommy Mars), and the differences in their styles (acoustic with Wolf and synthetic with Mars) is explored very well. The E Mixolydian solo is mostly unaccompanied, at first, and is an edit from a different performance. The note selection and composition of this solo is among Frank's best, and it's obvious why he chose this performance. He cleverly edits it to bring in a grander feel, bringing in the drummer at 4:02 after some synth fanfare. The addition of drum and bass kicks Frank into high gear, as Wolf plays piano beneath Frank.

Things peak at about 6:55 when Mars beautiful synth chords provide a backdrop for Frank's exploratory soloing. The stately approach favored by Mars here creates real emotion, one that Frank's critics always say he either lacked or faked. Mars seems to inspire Zappa even more, as he continues exploring beautiful melodies and sub-melodies. At 10:05, Frank starts playing one of the vocal themes, backed by Mars, to bring the solo section back to the original verse. The outro repeats the 'maybe you should stay with your mama' melody on multiple instruments with multiple singers, including the unmistakeable Moire, harmonizing before Frank's abrupt introduction of the band brings the song to a close.

Orchestral Favorites (1979)

Personnel:
Frank Zappa: guitar, keyboards, vocals
Mike Altschul: flute and clarinet
Terry Bozzio: drums
Bobby Dubow: violin
David Duke: French horn
Earle Dumler: oboe
Bruce Fowler: trombone
Pamela Goldsmith: viola
Dana Hughes: bass trombone
Jerry Kessler: cello
Mike Lang: keyboards
Joann McNab: bassoon
Malcolm McNab: trumpet
Dave Parlato: bass
Ray Reed: flute
Emil Richards: percussion
David Shostac: flute
John Wittenberg: violin
Michael Zearott: conductor
Producer: Frank Zappa
Recorded: September 19, 1975
Released: May 4, 1979
Peak Chart Position: Number 168 on the Billboard Top 200

The last *Lather*-related album was the second all-instrumental album of Zappa's career. Most of the original recordings were done four years before in a live setting with a 37-piece group. The most prominent members of this group are listed above. The group was named the Abnuceals Emuukha Electric Symphony Orchestra with Terry Bozzio on drums and Michael Zearott as conductor.

The grouping of these orchestral pieces makes sense and was probably the best decision Frank made when compiling the individual albums from the four-record set. The later release of the *Lather* box set by the Zappa Family Trust collected just three of these performances, though, so the album is essential. Though this may frustrate some modern buyers, the *Lather* track listing was created and prepared by Frank before his death and, therefore, conform to his wishes. All in all, this is his third album to feature a full orchestra and, in some ways, the purest expression of Zappa's classical writing up to that point.

Unfortunately, this performance was rushed, and preparation was minimal, resulting in mistakes. These types of errors plagued Zappa's orchestral work almost until the very end of his life. Overdubs help to fix some of these mistakes, though, and keep the work colorful. Rather than focus on composing new – and more complex – orchestral works, Zappa rearranged older tracks into a new format. As a result, *Orchestral Favorites* may be an easier entry into Zappa's classical world than the sprawling and baffling and patchwork – though excellent – *200 Motels* or the dense and challenging *London Symphony Orchestra* albums. Unfortunately, poor promotion – and public indifference to classical music – stalled the album's success and it was the least successful of Frank's many *Lather* projects. Unfortunately, contemporary reviews of the album are hard to find: the always tough Christgau only mentions it – disparagingly – in passing in his *Sleep Dirt* review, while modern reviews from sites like Allmusic gave it a solid three out of five stars and state that 'The themes are melodic and often majestic, with various startling juxtapositions and changes.' 'Classic Rock History' was very positive, saying: 'The arrangements, orchestrations, and performances are tight and played with the humor so closely associated with FZ's 'rock bands'...One of the most striking things about this CD is Zappa's genius for juxtaposition of musical styles, and of course, many parodies abound.'

Orchestral Favorites may be a Dark Horse in the Zappa catalog. Surrounded by dense rock material and, in many people's eyes, superseded by later orchestral releases, this album shouldn't be ignored. It's definitely the easiest of his orchestral works to understand.

'Strictly Genteel' (Frank Zappa)

Fans of *200 Motels* can rejoice at Frank's wise decision to take the beautiful closing piece from the parodic surrounding of the movie, strip away the juxtaposition into boogie rock, and focus strictly on the melodic and harmonic potential. Anyone who doubted Frank's ability to compose extended forms and melodic variations will experience surprise as he shows off his finesse. The opening piano part is all new and guides the orchestra, keyboards, and band through many melodic and harmonic changes. Multiple themes are stated and arranged with the skill of a top-tier Hollywood soundtrack composer. That is not an insult: Frank had the taste and talent to stand out in that field, should he have chosen it.

As the piece moves, the drama increases and horns become vital. The density of their harmonies and fast-paced melodies clash with what sounds like harmonica textures collapsing into semi-improvised sections. The strings flourish up and down the scales provides a semi-parodic counterpoint to the pomp of the piece. It is a grand start and one of the best performances on the album.

'Pedro's Dowry' (Frank Zappa)

This track appears on the boxset and is one of two composed for the project. Unlike the straight forward 'greatest hits' tracks on this album, 'Pedro's Dowry' is difficult. The immediately dissonant tone lets the listener know that everything isn't going to be peace and ease. The lithe percussion and orchestra during the opening show a dedication and skill from the performers that should be praised. Though the piece mostly plays 4/4, some polyrhythms exist. For example, parts include percussion and brass playing in 12/8 to create rhythmic complexity not surprising for Zappa. The listener can anticipate lapses into calm that resembles slightly disturbing chamber music. Then, bursts of aggression and dissonance pairs with an upbeat drum part by Bozzio to create tight dynamics. The version on *London Symphony Orchestra* follows the same pattern but with denser orchestration.

Beyond these types of arrangement tricks, Zappa also composes in a multitude of ways. Monodic music – a melody played as a single line or matched with parallel chords – mixes with rich harmonies that feature dense chords. A slight mixture of polyphonic playing, including horns playing independent but related lines, also appear. Small hocketing – instruments playing separate parts of a single melody – is also present but not as fully explored as Zappa would do in later orchestral works.

'Naval Aviation in Art?' (Frank Zappa)

Although this track is making its first appearance, Gail Zappa has said that its composition came as early as *200 Motels*. Though one of his shortest orchestral recordings, there is a purity of focus that helps it stand apart. The adagio aspect is consistent throughout giving the piece a sense of motion. The melody is built on a series of sustained tones that tweak every few bars with a barrage of 32nd notes to switch to the next chord. The unique construction continues the melody played via the fast notes with harmonization in sustained sections. The overall feeling is dissonance and atonality.

Each bar has new notes to sustain the momentum. It starts with Ab and D# sustained before adding a B to the melody. The sharped A is then flatted to a natural for the third bar before the B leaps to an E for the fourth. The fifth bar flats the natural A again before the sixth goes to E and back to a D. Frank adds harmony notes to increase the harmonic density, with F, E, C#, and D played as a chordal backing. Then, the Ab is sharpened to a natural A for the seventh bar with G, and C harmony notes backing the melody. Instruments continually change their notes in unpredictable ways to produce a one-of-a-kind effect unique for Frank's music.

'Duke of Prunes' (Frank Zappa)

The second side begins with this classic, which Frank had written as early as 1963. The original version from the *Run Home Slow* soundtrack has a small chamber feel to it and an almost jazz-like touch. This version expands upon the vocal version found on *Absolutely Free* and is played in a form that mimics, but does not mirror, a sonata. The first theme plays over a chordal backing that musicians have debated for years. On Zappa Analysis, the reviewer hears Fmaj9 and Em9 chords. Another reviewer states that the Fmaj9 chord is proper but the second chord is an F pedal F Lydian chord. These debates showcase the continued density and sophistication of Frank's music.

The construction of the piece includes the statement of three main themes. After they're done, Frank plays a related guitar solo over some basic chords. This solo is Frank's only guitar appearance though he does play some keyboard overdubs. The solo drops and the orchestra and guitar interact in an intermezzo format that shows Frank's mixture of rock and classical at its finest. The first theme returns and, interestingly, Frank foregoes further thematic development before jumping into a coda. 'Duke of Prunes' is the most straightforward track on the album but no less attractive for it. Subtle touches, such as falling into occasional triplet time, help to make this a fun piece.

Note: I'm not pointing out the many references and satirical pokes at various classical composers, such as Stravinsky and Mahler, as they are scattered so heavily throughout the album that they'd require a full chapter just to break them down. Clever listeners will enjoy catching these references though.

'Bogus Pomp' (Frank Zappa)

Fans of *200 Motels* will fall in love with this track, as it features much of the music from that film crammed into a 13-minute format. The later version on *London Symphony Orchestra* included more string parts for greater density and extended the length to over 20 minutes. This tauter version is just fine, though, and jumps into a barrage of string and percussion parts that set up a grand canvas on which Frank and the group can paint. Melodies come in from 'This Town is a Sealed Tuna Fish Sandwich,' and other parts of the score. Frank varies the themes and the tempos throughout, which makes 'spot that theme' a fun side quest while listening. The track rarely stays at a steady pace or volume, featuring extreme dynamic contrasts. One of Frank's composition tricks utilized here is the echoing of lines across various instruments.

This isn't quite the hocketing style used on *The Yellow Shark*. Instead, this sound comes when one instrument plays a brief passage (often no more than a few chords) that is echoed by another instrument playing the same melody. Listen carefully, and you can hear it heavily here. Sustained notes feature heavily, linking some of its textures to 'Naval Aviation in Art?' but without the same techniques. Anticipate more variations on the 'Tuna Sandwich' theme with tweaks to the pedal notes, including changes from D to a G that create varying harmonic textures. The end result is one of Frank's best orchestral pieces, no matter the version.

Joe's Garage (1979)

Personnel:
Frank Zappa: lead guitar, vocals
Warren Cuccurullo: rhythm guitar, vocals
Denny Walley: slide guitar, vocals
Ike Willis: lead vocals
Peter Wolf: keyboards
Tommy Mars: keyboards
Arthur Barrow: bass guitar, guitar (on 'Joe's Garage'), vocals
Patrick O'Hearn: bass guitar on 'Outside Now' and 'He Used to Cut the Grass'
Ed Mann: percussion, vocals
Vinnie Colaiuta: drums, combustible vapors, optometric abandon
Jeff (Jeff Hollie): tenor sax
Marginal Chagrin (Earle Dumler): baritone sax
Stumuk (Bill Nugent): bass sax
Dale Bozzio: vocals
Al Malkin: vocals
Craig Steward: harmonica
Producer: Frank Zappa
The Cast
Frank Zappa – Central Scrutinizer, Larry, L. Ron Hoover, Father Riley & Buddy Jones
Ike Willis: Joe
Dale Bozzio: Mary
Denny Walley: Mrs. Borg
Al Malkin: Officer Butzis
Warren Cuccurullo & Ed Mann: Sy Borg
Terry Bozzio: Bald-Headed John
The Utility Muffin Research Kitchen Chorus – Al Malkin, Warren Cucurullo, Dale Bozzio, Geordie Hormel, Barbara Issak & most of the people who work at Village Recorders
Recorded: March through June 1979
Released: Act I September 17, 1979, Acts II and III November 19, 1979
Peak Chart Position: Act I, Number 27 on the Billboard Top 200: Acts II-III, Number 53 on the Billboard Top 200

After the creative work of the *Lather* period, Frank Zappa could be forgiven if he didn't necessarily put in his A-game for the followup. And, for some – particularly critics at the time – *Joe's Garage* was likely a letdown. For some, it was probably the first letdown and for others – like perennial Zappa-basher Robert Christgau – *Joe's Garage* was very likely just the last in a long line of disappointments.

The music was a further step away from the intricate jazz-classical-rock fusions Zappa pursued during the '70s and was an embrace, in parts, of rock- or pop-oriented styles. The lyrics were filthier than ever over a triple-album length presented as a rock opera with a real libretto that detailed the character's singing. The story was mostly held together by all bodily fluids rather than raw logic. The third record was the toughest sell: an LP of 'imaginary guitar solos' with minimal dialogue or singing that ends with the inane 'Little Green Rosetta,' which brings the whole thing to a grinding halt that could feel dissatisfying and which may have put off many fans for life. The 'blackface' on the cover, amazingly, rarely gets mentioned in reviews. Yowza, yowza, yowza!

The strange thing about this album is that it thrives in an environment that seemed to promise nothing but 'cheap thrills' and rises into rarefied air as, not only one of Zappa's finest records of the '70s but one of his very best ever. This time, a majority of fans and critics alike are – mostly – unified in their love. For example, Don Shewey of *Rolling Stone* wrote, 'If the surface of this opera is cluttered with cheap gags and musical mishmash, its soul is located in profound existential sorrow. The guitar solos that Zappa plays in Joe's imagination burn with a desolate, devastating beauty. Flaws and all, *Joe's Garage* is Frank Zappa's *Apocalypse Now*.' High praise indeed! The opera also received 4.5 out of 5 stars from Steve Huey of Allmusic, who wrote: '...Joe's Garage has enough substance to make it one of Zappa's most important '70s works and overall political statements...,' and *Modern Drummer* magazine ranked the album as one of the top 25 greatest drumming performances and named Vinnie Colaiuta as 'the most technically advanced drummer ever.'

Not bad for an album that started as nothing more than a single – 'Joe's Garage' backed with 'Catholic Girls.' As he worked, he and the band jammed out lengthy and knotty tunes that he successfully edited into this album using xenochrony. Vinnie would improvise new drum parts to these mixed-up pieces. And as he started to write lyrics, he found that they were connected by a common theme: fear of control by the government, the stupidity of the government, and music being stymied by the government. Zappa wrote a very quick story based around Joe's fall from grace thanks to laws that haven't yet been written and releases his second great satirical album. This thematic focus gave the album a natural flow and, on the thin story, Zappa drapes multiple genres, incredible ensemble playing, catchy pop songs, intricate arrangements, xenochrony, and some beautiful and heartfelt guitar soloing. All of these elements work to create a sustained bit of anguish, a tortured, blackly comedic masterpiece that is unlike anything he ever produced.

Joe's Garage is a cry against the loss of individuality and intelligent thought that Frank saw overtaking the world. And listening to the melodies – and this album is filled with a rich array of emotional tones and textures – makes it clear that the album was a very serious one for Frank, one in which he – obliquely – lays bare his soul for the world to see, perhaps more than he ever had on any other album. Though songs like 'Joe's Garage,' 'Catholic Girls,' and 'Why Does It Hurt When I Pee?' may have a satirical lyrical and musical bent, their melodies remain effective and showcase the desperation Frank may have felt in the face of such – what he thought were – rapidly worsening times. The straight melodies bend to convention for a reason: Frank wants to hit the emotions of his listeners and to get them to understand the importance of his cultural criticisms and, perhaps, move them to change. The most obvious example of this emotional honesty is the poem near the end of the album, what I call Zappa's Creed. This bit of insightful – and beautiful – poetry tells you more about Frank than any autobiography of the man ever will:

Information is not knowledge
Knowledge is not wisdom
Wisdom is not truth
Truth is not beauty
Beauty is not love
Love is not music
Music is THE BEST

'Central Scrutinizer' (Frank Zappa)
The musical's thesis gets introduced, as does the narrator 'The Central Scrutinizer.' Played by Frank whispering through a megaphone, this character enforces all the laws that haven't been written yet. He describes how rock music is so damaging and sets up the story: the whole album is a lengthy PSA by a totalitarian government. The music is a vamp that eventually becomes more involved. The percussion parts play a handsome melody before the vamp is faded. The vamp is surprisingly complex, with D Mixolydian in the first bar, D Dorian in the next, and a jump in major seconds with the marimbas.

'Joe's Garage' (Frank Zappa)
We are introduced to our main character, Joe and his rock band. This song is, in my opinion, the finest ode to rock ever written. Rather than the 'fist to the sky and scream' anthems you get from so many bands, Frank writes about his garage band with nostalgia – things were so much simpler then – while mocking the actual music quality. Frank isn't fooling anyone – rock is dumb, and he knows it. The music mostly plays a simple I-IV-V progression and features Ike Willis as Joe. The recurrence of the 'stupid riff' on guitar and saxophone throughout is funny: it is the kind of riff you can imagine a beginning rock band playing. Reality intrudes as the band gets a little success before being ripped off by their record label, and Joe is arrested for being too loud.

'Catholic Girls' (Frank Zappa)
Frank takes things up a notch with this track, which features conventional chords (I-IV-I-VI-V) varied with melodic and harmonic intensity. For example, he moves through C# Dorian, Gb Lydian, Db Dorian, Ab Mixolydian, E Dorian, and much more all before 1:30 has passed. Vinnie is a beast who moves through the themes with grace and fluidity. Even when things slow down for Ike to sing about the joy of having sex with Catholic girls, Vinnie remains taut.

The lyrics here mock the 'virtuous' reputation the Catholic church tried to set and tries to show that the girls here are like any other – interested in sex.

'Crew Slut' (Frank Zappa)
At this point, the girl Mary whom Joe has fallen for ends up on a rock band's touring bus. The verses have an F-E-D and A-C-A vamp with the bass playing a D pedal note. The chorus includes Frank talking over the top like a roadie trying to get a girl into bed. The 'I'll buy you a pizza' line seems particularly sleazy. And while Mary – and other girls – are portrayed as being quite dumb, Frank also mocks the perverted nature of the crew. The instrumentation of guitar, harmonica, and what sounds like a sitar creates a wheezy and sleazy atmosphere that fits the song perfectly. Mary, stuck with the band, needs money to get home and how she gets it is described in the next track.

'Fembot in a Wet T-Shirt' (Frank Zappa)
During this track, the music takes on a fairly light and silly tone. The cheesy music is appropriate: Frank is detailing a wet t-shirt night. Joe is thrilled but less than enthused when Mary suddenly shows up. The music features the same sudden mood changes common throughout Zappa's music, including a dark and twisted piece of music led by that weirdly persistent sitar, tuned percussion, and sharp guitar. The verse is propelled by funk-style syncopation and occasional bursts of mock-heroic keyboard and sitar lines. The alternation of these genres, including the ridiculous build to the 'wet ones, big wet ones' line is laugh-out-loud hilarious, much like Frank's impersonation of a wet t-shirt contest operator. The way he pronounces 'here's your $50 bucks' lets you know exactly what he thinks.

'On the Bus' (Frank Zappa)
The first overt act of xenochrony features a Frank solo later released as 'Occam's Razor' overdubbed over another backing track. The result feels fluent and attractive, but the xenochrony throws the tune off-kilter in a good way. The uneasy feeling fits the mood, as what we've experienced so far is a strange and emotional turn of events. Bursts of electric sitar pop up again

'Why Does It Hurt When I Pee?' (Frank Zappa)
Joe has fallen into disarray because of Mary's abandonment and seeks solace in the bed of another. However, he catches a 'disease with an unpronounceable name' and laments his condition in this amazing song. The music is a mockery of the sort of pseudo-prog common at the time: ridiculous 'heroic' guitar lines, constant buildups, massed chorals, simple riffs, and a sense of exaggerated importance. The fact that the song's music outclasses most fake prog songs put together makes it even better, as does Ike's straight and impassioned performance. One feels that Frank – a very sexually active man – could relate

to this song's message quite well, though one can also lament that he did have affairs with other women against his wife Gail's wishes.

'Lucille Has Messed My Mind Up' (Frank Zappa)
This startling track is something Frank claimed he'd never write: a sentimental love ballad. Joe is heartbroken over the loss of the woman who gave him the disease and laments that fact over a simple, but effective, reggae rhythm. The band plays 4/4 and 12/8 at the same time, creating a light form of polyrhythmic complexity. This variation never calls attention to itself but feels natural and relaxed. Ike is the star of the track and album, as he sells the simple lyrical concept over the basic music in a dedicated manner.

'Scrutinizer Postlude' (Frank Zappa)
This track was originally part of the previous song on the vinyl copy but has a separate CD index. Frank whispers through the megaphone and discusses how confused Joe has become and how he fell into various forms of religion, specifically the Church of Appliantology run by L. Ron Hoover.

'A Token of My Extreme' (Frank Zappa)
The first song on Act II is an older track, versions of which appeared during the Roxy era mixed with 'Tush, Tush, Tush.' Frank sings significant portions, backed up by his guitar playing the main melody. The lyrics come from the perspective of L. Ron Hoover, a very obvious parody of sci-fi writer turned religious guru L. Ron Hubbard. The music changes when Joe sings, as he laments his suffering and his sexual confusion. Ike does a great job moving through some very silly lyrics and difficult melodies: even when he gets labeled a 'latent appliance fetishist,' Ike as Joe takes things quite well. Joe chooses a German sexbot – of course – and gives L. Ron Hoover $50 for his advice.

'Stick It Out' (Frank Zappa)
Joe tries to seduce the sexbot, starting out in (terrible) German set to a disco arrangement. The melody here is insanely catchy and among one of Frank's finest earworms. Singing along to 'fuck me you ugly son of a bitch' is one of the best moments on the whole album. And, satirically, the dig at fetishists is appropriate enough to make the track fun. Could Frank have been a disco-pop star? Who knows?

Historical note: Originally, this track was part of the lengthy 'sofa suite' all the way back in 1971.

'Sy Borg' (Frank Zappa)
This nine-minute long track plays like a standard R&B ballad. The tempo is slow, Vinnie's drumming is excellent, the keyboards are electric, and Ike sings like a demented Luther Vandross. The melody here is quite good, backed by

Frank's reggae guitar and bursts of electric piano and synthesizers. Were it not for the lyrics, this could have been a hit. The lyrics focus on Joe's seduction of the sexbot, but Joe gets a little too excited and kills the robot with his 'plooking.' Having no more money – having been fleeced by Hoover two songs ago – Joe is arrested by The Central Scrutinizer to 'pay his duty,' if you will, to the government.

'Dong Work for Yuda' (Frank Zappa)
The second side of the second act starts in some pretty disturbing areas. Joe is arrested and sent to a jail for 'musicians and former executives' who take turns 'snorting detergent and plooking each other.' Frank drops character here, turns off the megaphone, and laughs. The bass is the most prominent instrument locked into a groove with Vinnie, who remains a perfectly wild drummer. This simple blues stays in E major with a mixed Mixolydian. The track is gross if you pay attention to the lyrics, but appropriate for the track. Best not to think about it too much.

'Keep It Greasy' (Frank Zappa)
Another older track (1976), 'Keep It Greasy' gets something of a definitive reading. Vinnie is a madman, bashing out a semi-disco-funk rhythm to which Arthur Barrow plays beautiful bass in a fluent but exaggerated manner. The sitar pops up during the chorus, matching the 'keep it greasy' vocal melody. The track has a pretty chaotic sound that may be hard for some to handle. Vinnie's drumming is partially to blame but not in a bad way. He was Keith Moon-ish in his approach, which I dig. Strange musicality pops up in a 19/16 vamp during Frank's guitar solo. This instrumental texture distracts the listener from the fact that they're singing about keeping objects greasy to make intercourse easier.

'Outside Now' (Frank Zappa)
Act II ends with one of the best melodies Frank ever wrote. Though in a basic Bb Lydian, Frank varies the meter in a 6/8 and 5/8 to make the rhythm slightly off-kilter. The simple arpeggios provide a beautiful backing for Ike to lament as Joe. There's a real sense of sorrow as Joe sings about getting 'plooked' by executives while wanting to make his guitar sing. Joe decides to become withdrawn and dream of guitar notes. Frank then plays a jagged and atonal solo that would definitely 'annoy an executive type of guy.' The track goes into a lengthy singalong with Ike and other voices singing 'I can't wait to see what it's like to see on the outside now.' The melody is beautiful and full of promise and menace: what it's like on the outside might not be quite what Joe hopes for but he's still ready to get out as soon as possible. The ending melody makes that quite clear, as it's full of dissonance, uncertainty, and unpredictable burst of rhythm noise.

Note: Frank later played guitar solos based on this melody and even turned the guitar solo into a Synclavier composition later.

'He Used to Cut the Grass' (Frank Zappa)

At the start of Act III, Joe has finally gotten out of prison and laments the fact that there's nothing fun to do now that music is illegal. Ike believably sings this track and having to find a way to express yourself. Joe goes back to the sullen and withdrawn lifestyle he'd pursued while in prison and dreams of guitar solos that 'go with the loading zone announcement.' Frank cuts loose with a guitar solo that sprawls in a focused way. Sticking to E Lydian – with a brief switch to F# Mixolydian – Frank plays sharp and stinging licks that express Joe's trauma. Flashbacks to a woman screaming 'he used to cut my grass, he was a nice boy' from the title track come back before the Scrutinizer lectures:

> Now his mind is totally destroyed by music. He's so crazy now he even believes that people are writing articles and reviews about his imaginary guitar notes. And so, continuing to dwindle in the twilight realm of his own secret thoughts, he not only dreams imaginary guitar notes but to make matters worse, dreams imaginary vocal parts to a song about the imaginary journalistic profession.

'Packard Goose' (Frank Zappa)

This might be the most 'real' song on the third act, and while Frank keeps the melody very simple (dianoetic), he switches around a few bars by swapping an A with an A#. Ike sings as Joe singing as Frank:

> All them rock n roll writers is the worst kind of sleaze
> Selling punk like some new kinda English disease
> Is that the wave of the future? Aw, spare me, please!

Coals to Newcastle, perhaps, but the vitriol in the song's lyrics match the music, which is a fairly stomping bit of heavy rock. Joe rallies against the rock and roll critics whom he (Frank) believed knew nothing about music before things shift to a softer and gentler direction. Mary suddenly makes an appearance to narrate the poem about 'music being the best.' A dramatic change to more heavy rock music – almost a satire of such dramatic moments in rock operas – heralds a new vamp over which Zappa solos. His licks cut like a knife, particularly if the music poem gives you goosebumps. The solo ends with an abrupt slam back into the sung melody. A lengthy singalong over the last two minutes gives listeners a flash forward to the album end.

'Watermelon in Easter Hay' (Frank Zappa)

The Central Scrutinizer comes back to discuss Joe's depression, knowing that the 'end is near' and that 'imaginary guitar notes and imaginary vocals only exist in the imagination of the imaginer.' Zappa then cracks up before one last guitar solo. This represents the last guitar solo Joe will ever dream. And Frank hits it out of the park. Though the vamping chords are fairly simple – and the harmonies not incredibly complex – Frank goes for a style he'd rarely touched upon in the past: pure emotion. Yes, the 'big emotional guitar solo' is a cliché in rock operas and Frank had to satirize it by writing the end-all-be-all of solos. Slight rhythmic shenanigans (6/8+5/8) don't detract from the stinging sustain or the melodic moves Frank makes. Rather than sprawling all over the fretboard – in admittedly usually fascinating ways – he focuses on exploring a melody and mood to its fullest. And I'll be damned if he – with fine support from the backing musicians, particularly Vinnie – doesn't do just that here.

Could this solo simply be an emulation of beautiful playing? Perhaps. However, it is easier to believe that Frank just let himself express his emotions more fully, giving free rein to what he minimized or compressed in his music. If so, it's sad that he didn't explore this level of emotion more often. As heard here, he was very good at it.

'A Little Green Rosetta' (Frank Zappa)

After the emotional peaks of the last track, the Central Scrutinizer comes back to tell us that yes, this story was sad, but that's what happens when you break the law. Frank puts down the megaphone and leads the band through a singalong of 'A Little Green Rosetta,' a tune teased on *Lather*. However, this version goes for a full eight minutes and 14 seconds and is quite silly. Expect a lot of tuned percussion, sterling Vinnie drumming, and a large number of people singing on the chorus. The musicians react to Frank well, which causes him to sing 'pretty good musicians' to the main theme.

What a bizarre and very Zappa-like way to end such an album. Rather than trying to hit the 'universal' chord, he deflates the mood and laughs at himself and his pretensions to give the audience something dumb and fun to sing. How else would Zappa end this serious project?

What Happened After *Joe's Garage*?

Although this book ends in 1979, Frank's career was far from over. The 1980s were a very busy time for him in multiple musical forms. In 1981 alone, he released five albums: the hit-and-miss live album *Tinsel Town Rebellion*, the three volumes of *Shut Up 'n Play Yer Guitar*, and his last rock album masterpiece *You Are What You Is*. The latter album was a return to high-quality satire and featured tight editing, clever melodies, and dense arrangements.

Frank started to separate from rock and roll during this period, releasing the short *Ship Arriving Too Late to Save a Drowning Witch* in 1982, which featured his fluke hit with daughter Moon, 'Valley Girl.' The rest of the album was dense, treble-heavy, and very strange rock with no precedent in his earlier work. *The Man From Utopia* featured simpler songs and a focus on a strange 'guitarspeak' composition style that featured Steve Vai matching Frank's spoken monologue with his guitar playing.

1983 was when Frank started moving into orchestral music, with the first volume of *London Symphony Orchestra* being released in this year. But 1984 was, perhaps, his most productive year ever: he released a classical album conducted by Pierre Boulez (*The Perfect Stranger*) that combined orchestral music and his first experiments with the Synclavier. He then produced a Synclavier album of classical music written by a baroque composer named 'Francesco Zappa,' his final totally rock-based album, the double *Them or Us*, and a sprawling three-record (!) rock opera, *Thing-Fish*.

After this burst of creativity, Frank focused entirely on Synclavier and orchestral music, putting out several albums of each as the 80s progressed. He also continued to collect old live material to release on various archive albums, including the *You Can't Do That On Stage Anymore* series. Touring was not a prominent goal at this point, though political action became an important part of his life.

This new career focus started with the PMRC meetings in 1985, during which Frank testified against the measure. He commemorated this experience with *Frank Zappa Meets the Mothers of Prevention* in 1985. And he also became a very heavy proponent for voting, often urging his listeners to register to vote and even opening up booths where they could do just that at his concerts.

In 1988, he put together a monster live band for what turned out to be his last tour. The personnel on tour was vast and talented, and the music produced was some of his most diverse, mature, and engaging in years. Unfortunately, interpersonal squabbling squashed the tour early, though three live albums (*Broadway the Hard Way*, *The Best Band You Never Heard in Your Life*, and *Make a Jazz Noise Here*), a few DVDs, and bootlegs compiled different elements of the band's approach.

Unfortunately, two years later, he was diagnosed with prostate cancer. The condition had been developing for ten years and was not operable at that point. As a result, Frank started working even harder, sometimes through very intense pain. Some of the finest material of his life appeared during this time, including the dense *The Yellow Shark* played by the German chamber group Ensemble Modern. Frank, and many fans consider it the best of his orchestral works due to the accuracy and dedication of the group.

While his cancer progressed throughout 1992 and 1993, Zappa worked feverishly on several projects, including a compilation of rare tracks entitled *The Lost Episodes* and his Synclavier masterwork, *Civilization Phaze III*. This album showcased his composition techniques at their purest and wildest and is one of his most successful serious works.

Since his death on December 4, 1993, the Zappa Family Trust has released more than 50 albums showcasing different elements of his work. These include live shows, completed albums Frank never released in his lifetime, and much more. And the future appears to promise much more great work. As Varese said (and which Frank quoted many times), 'the present-day composer refuses to die.'

Also from Sonicbond Publishing

On Track series
Queen Andrew Wild 978-1-78952-003-3
Emerson Lake and Palmer Mike Goode 978-1-78952-000-2
Deep Purple and Rainbow 1968-79 Steve Pilkington 978-1-78952-002-6
Yes Stephen Lambe 978-1-78952-001-9
Blue Oyster Cult Jacob Holm-Lupo 978-1-78952-007-1
The Beatles Andrew Wild 978-1-78952-009-5
Roy Wood and the Move James R Turner 978-1-78952-008-8
Genesis Stuart MacFarlane 978-1-78952-005-7
Jethro Tull Jordan Blum 978-1-78952-016-3
The Rolling Stones 1963-80 Steve Pilkington 978-1-78952-017-0
Judas Priest John Tucker 978-1-78952-018-7
Toto Jacob Holm-Lupo 978-1-78952-019-4
Van Der Graaf Generator Dan Coffey 978-1-78952-031-6
Frank Zappa 1966 to 1979 Eric Benac 978-1-78952-033-0
Elton John in the 1970s Peter Kearns 978-1-78952-034-7
The Moody Blues Geoffrey Feakes 978-1-78952-042-2
The Beatles Solo 1969-1980 Andrew Wild 978-1-78952-042-2
Steely Dan Jez Rowden 978-1-78952-043-9
Pink Floyd Solo Mike Goode 978-1-78952-046-0
Hawkwind Duncan Harris 978-1-78952-043-9
Fairport Convention Kevan Furbank 978-1-78952-052-1
Iron Maiden Steve Pilkington 978-1-78952-061-3

On Screen series
Carry On... Stephen Lambe 978-1-78952-004-0
Powell and Pressburger Sam Proctor 978-1-78952-013-2
Seinfeld Seasons 1 to 5 Stephen Lambe 978-1-78952-012-5
Francis Ford Coppola Cam Cobb and Stephen Lambe 978-1-78952-022-4
Breaking Bad Roman Colombo 978-1-78952-045-3
Monty Python Steve Pilkington 978-1-78952-047-7

Other Books
Not As Good As The Book Andy Tillison 978-1-78952-021-7
The Voice. Frank Sinatra in the 1940s Stephen Lambe 978-1-78952-032-3
Maximum Darkness Deke Leonard 978-1-78952-048-4
The Twang Dynasty Deke Leonard 978-1-78952-049-1
Maybe I Should've Stayed In Bed Deke Leonard 978-1-78952-053-8

and many more to come!